Comfort for the Tears

Trigger warning:
This book contains sensitive photographs and stories that you may find upsetting. Please be respectful of each photograph along with the story. These stories are factual and are written by people who have experenced complications before, during and after pregnancy.

To all the families that have:
Grieved for the loss of their baby or infant during or
after pregnancy
Felt heartache after their baby was born too early
Struggled to fall pregnant

This book is dedicated to you

God

Didn't promise days without

Pain

Laughter

without **Sorrow**

nor **Sun** *without*

Rain *But he did promise*

Strength

for the day

Comfort

for the **Tears** *and*

Light

for the way

Contents

Forward

Toward the end of October 2018, I received a message from Melissa who was inquiring about editing services. She explained that she was looking to release a compilation of pregnancy stories, some of which had already been published in her first book, Comfort for the tears, Light for the way. The terms were standard, nothing I wasn't used to. She made it clear she had only her contributor's best interests at heart; she was adamant that because of the sensitivity of the stories, she wanted very little altered. "They are true stories," she'd told me, "so the writers are being extremely vulnerable in sharing them."

Sensitivity? Vulnerable?

It was then it clicked that these were stories contributed by heartbroken families who'd stepped out of their comfort zones and broken their silence in order to share their struggles with the world, to have their voices heard, to have their babies honored, and to wrap their arms around others with similar stories. All in one instant, the breath was knocked from my lungs and for a moment, I forgot how to breathe.

I paused and took a few minutes before I replied to Melissa's message. I had to. I didn't doubt that I could edit the stories in a manner that left the authors' messages intact. I'm pretty good leaving the original tone and voice of the works I edit alone. But, did I have what it would take to make it through all the stories in a professional manner?

I answered Melissa's request with the basic editor reply. I explained how I worked, the steps we would take in terms of editing, and what she could expect from me as an editor. I sent the message, tossed my editor hat out of the window, and followed that message with a more personal one. "By the way, I'm a mama of five along with three angel babies I never got to meet."

And there it was. It was too late to take back. It wasn't at all professional and it was way outside the boundaries of business and what she was hiring me for. Yet she embraced me for it, the way only someone who has suffered their own tragedy can.

In fact, it wasn't until we began the editing process that I learned her story. What heartache and pain she'd endured. And then other stories were sent, and I wept—openly, ugly-crying—wept for each of the families. I felt their pain then and I feel it now. I sobbed through their losses and shouted out loud for their victories.

Yes, their victories. Each family dealt with their loss and sought healing in their own way. They've honored the babies they've laid to rest and gave a voice to their trauma. Some had other children later on and some didn't. Some chose to foster children stuck in the system and give them happy homes. Some went on to pursue an education and career relating directly to their experiences with grief so that they could be a blessing to someone else in pain.

Regardless of the paths they chose, all of them had a common thread between them: to keep their little ones alive in memory, to speak their names and their existences—no matter how brief—and to carry that life with them always. And that, to me, is true victory.

There was another theme I noticed in several of the stories, one I feel relevant to this foreword so that those reading this book that haven't gone through these types of experiences will be aware of. One of the most awful feelings in life is to suffer a great loss and feel like you are being avoided because of it, or to feel like you can't talk about it with those around you.

Even if you can't relate to the experience, you can listen. Sometimes that's all we want. An ear. A shoulder. Someone to vent our anger to. Someone to hand us a tissue. Someone who won't turn around and walk the other way because they can't stand to see the hurt in our faces.

I suffered two of three miscarriages by myself; alone. There was no one to talk to. The three or four people who knew thought it better to ignore the experience and suggested I do the same. I didn't want to move on. I didn't want to ignore what I'd lost. I wanted my losses recognized. I wanted someone—anyone—to sit and listen when I needed it, someone to tell me I didn't have to "get over it and move on."

Not knowing what to say is okay. Ignoring someone's pain is not. Grief should be released, not repressed.

To all the families who were so brave and courageous in their contributions to this book, I admire each and every one of you. I am so honored to have been able to read your stories and help you edit them. You have walked through your own personal hells and found your way back. You genuinely and truly amaze me and I adore you all. Your strength and perseverance will be torches to light the way for others still struggling in the darkness of grief. Thank you for your precious light.

To those suffering, take solace in this book. Find comfort in its pages. No one can tell you how to process your grief; it is unique to you and you only. But know that there are others out there who have stood in your shoes and cried your tears. Their arms ache to hold angels just like yours ache. You are not alone, and I promise, there is still hope.

Jody E. Freeman

Introduction

Comfort for the Tears is a collection of heartbreaking and heartwarming memoirs of pregnancy. These memoirs are written by families that have experienced the loss of a baby through pregnancy or after birth, premature births or had struggles falling pregnant.

This book was first released in October 2016, originally called Comfort for the tears, Light for the way.

It was such a transformational journey for me to help families around the world share their experiences of pregnancy and infant loss, fertility troubles, and premature births. I would never have thought that bringing a book of relatable stories to life would be needed. I was wrong. Families needed support and guidance; sometimes even the most supportive person in their life won't understand what they are experiencing.

When Comfort for the tears, Light for the way was released, I could not have been happier to see all the authors receive their books and read their own story. It was life changing for them as much as it was for me. Holding a book in your hand that you have published is a feeling that cannot be described. I suppose the feeling is different for everyone, but for me, it was pure excitement!

Writing is a powerful way to help heal the heart. It's a therapeutic way to self discovery and creates a clear view of what one can achieve. Sharing a story with the world opens the doors of opportunity.

I wrote my very first book called My life of Loss after my second son was born. It tells the story of my life, having experienced three miscarriages and giving birth to my stillborn daughter. It was a period of my life that left me so heartbroken that I didn't believe I was capable of ever having living children.

After I released My life of Loss, that door of opportunity suddenly burst opened. I told a story of the most difficult time of my life and people heard. I was given an opportunity to speak, write articles, have my story written about in the media, and I became a better, wiser and a more confident person for it.

It was apparent to me that more people needed to read and write about their own pregnancy journeys, so after I gave an opportunity to people on my Facebook page, I was inundated with requests to write their stories. These stories became Comfort for the tears, Light for the way. I couldn't seem to find many other books of its kind so it felt right to share these memoirs in one book.

I knew that this book could help thousands of people. My vision is to continue to help people with a personal story write it, so they too can empower, inspire, and provide support and guidance to other people and families globally.

Over the last three years, I've been involved in self development and starting my own business helping people write their own story so they can self publish it. Through all my experiences, I decided it was time to re-release Comfort for Tears, making a few changes including the name, cover, and adding new stories.

Every day, I jump on Facebook and see another post that a baby was stillborn or a mother has miscarried. These people rush to the support groups, wanting to know the answers to questions that come from grief. It breaks my heart.

There are hundreds of support groups and organisations in the world and if it weren't for them, there wouldn't be special events such as the yearly Pregnancy and Infant Loss Awareness Day that is held internationally or fundraisers to support the parents while their baby is in intensive care. These and many other people try hard to help bring such a taboo subject to light and support families in need so they don't have to struggle with grief alone.

The honest truth is that everyone deals with grief differently, and there is no right or wrong way to deal with it. What one person can say to a grieving person may not feel right for them. Suggesting that they write their feelings down in a way that makes sense to them can not only help them understand their own feelings, but share their understanding and grief with others too.

I've asked hundreds of questions in these groups and collected information. When I ask, "Why do you want to write your story?"the most common answer I receive is that they want to help other people and they wished they'd had a book like this to read when they were grieving.

Comfort for the Tears is not a book that will give you the answers to your questions of pregnancy struggles or another self-help workbook. It's a book written by courageous families sharing their stories to support you, guide you, and help you understand that you don't have to go through your grief alone.

Comfort for the Tears is a way of giving the world an opportunity to hold onto one book, to share an understanding, to show compassion, and empathise with these families that have endured pregnancy struggles. Most of all, it's an opportunity to believe in hope and happiness in your own lives.

Melissa Desveaux

Contributing Authors

Compiled & Published by Melissa Desveaux

Jean-Francois Desveaux
Tara Watson
Jeanette Buhagiar
Christine McKenna
Shalina Johnson
Martina Vassallo
Alicia Sinfield
Erin Johnson
Annaleise and Kyle Williams
Maree Grindrod
Danielle Nix
Janice Dufficy
Rebecca Riggio
Naomi Carpinteri
Meekehleh Maree Connors
Dani Buckley
Jenny Tiernan
Natalie Panetta
Jessica Burdus
Zena Mason
Meredith Bale
Carolyn Viera

Thank you for your contributions

My Life of Loss & Love

As I lay on the bed in the ultrasound room one morning in October 2007, I was hoping and praying my baby would be okay. The blood I saw earlier worried me.

The jelly felt cold as the lady searched for a heartbeat. She left the room, looking for a doctor to check me.

I waited alone in a large, open room for the results. But I already knew. The doctor walked up to me, kneeled down to my level, and gently told me my baby had passed.

I was just eight weeks pregnant. The only emotion I knew at that moment was disbelief.

I walked to the bathroom, closed the door, and cried as I called my husband to tell him what I had just learned.

That was the beginning of my life of loss.

In April 2008, I laid on another ultrasound bed. The lady used a Doppler to check the size of my baby. This time, I was eighteen weeks. She performed the usual ultrasound procedures and to me, it looked like my baby was fine. We could see her moving around and we were excited to see her! However, the lady was concerned that my baby wasn't the size she should have been at that gestational age. She was two weeks behind.

Maybe she is just small, we thought. We started to worry. Why was this happening to us?

My doctor referred me to Sydney Ultrasound for Women to see a foetal management specialist. More tests and visits to not only our obstetrician but also a professor. We traveled to the city just to see him over a period of nine weeks.

Those weeks were filled with stress and worry. Physically and mentally, my husband and I were drained.

I had many blood tests done, including an amniocentesis to rule out any abnormalities, and they all came back normal.

I was about twenty-one weeks pregnant. The scans still showed little growth in our baby's development, so the specialist decided to wait a week to see if there was an improvement.

There was little at our next scan. The specialist was very concerned about the health of our baby and suggested waiting another three weeks, hoping to see a dramatic change.

The end to the long wait of three weeks finally arrived. I was in the twenty-fifth week of pregnancy—but my baby wasn't growing. She wasn't being nourished and there was nothing I could do.

The three of us sat in the doctor's room, a box of tissues on a small table in front of us as the doctor explained the problem. I had placenta inefficiency and my baby was just two hundred and ninety-six grams at twenty-seven weeks pregnant.

And then came the words no parent wants to hear: "You have two options; you can either terminate the pregnancy or just let nature take its course."

We were devastated! After one miscarriage, I wasn't prepared to lose another baby.

Our specialist told us that if our baby grew to about six hundred grams by week thirty, we might have a chance of early delivery by C-section. We left with heavy hearts all the way home. There was nothing we could do—it was all up to our baby.

Our next scan at the twenty-seventh week showed there was no fluid in the sac and the baby now only weighed three hundred and twenty grams. It seemed unlikely our baby would grow another three hundred grams in the next three weeks.

Our specialist told us that there was no chance our baby would survive. He said that the baby was too small to be delivered and in a couple of weeks, her heart would just stop beating. He offered to see me every week to check the baby's progress.

Although we had prior warning, the pain and agony of knowing our baby would not survive was unbearable. We were hoping for some sort of miracle.

A week later was the last night I felt my baby kick. I used a Doppler to check our baby's heartbeat. It was one hundred and fifty-two beats per minute. When I woke the next morning, I checked for a heartbeat again and there wasn't one. I was a little worried, and suspected that it would be the day that would change our life.

I had a doctor's appointment the same day, and as I again

lay on the ultrasound bed, he searched for a heartbeat. There wasn't one.

"Sorry love, it looks like the baby has already passed," were the doctor's words.

"Okay. What now?" I was not shocked; in fact, I was quite calm. He then checked my cervix. After us asking, our doctor told us that our baby is a little girl.

I cried. My husband cried. We were heartbroken.
Our doctor said that we were to go to hospital.

Leaving our doctor, we then called our parents, gave them the news, and said that we were on our way to the hospital to keep an eye on my blood pressure and to prepare for being induced the next morning. Our whole family came to see us that night.

After a concoction of medication and being induced for the next twenty-four hours, I started to labour. I was in extreme pain.

The midwife checked my cervix, and I was dilated about three centimeters at that point. My husband stayed up with me until about 3am to give me gas, then went to sleep while I was resting. I couldn't move and had to stay in one position all night with pain in my lower back.

At around 7:30am on 27 June 2008, I was taken back to my room, and our doctor came in at about 8am. He checked my cervix again. I was in a lot of pain at that point. He asked me to push a few times and our baby, a little girl, was born at 8:08am. We named her Charlize. The placenta came out a few minutes later, and the pain in my back was completely gone.

There was no sound in the room. My husband was in shock, and the midwife was weeping as she watched Charlize being born.

My little baby girl lay lifeless in front of me. As I sat up to see her, all I could feel at that moment was sorrow.

After Charlize was bathed, the midwife brought her back to us. I held her in my arms and kissed her forehead. She was so little.

The midwife took prints of Charlize's feet and hands. We were given a teddy bear, blanket, beanie, and booties. A priest came in to bless Charlize. Our hearts ached as we gently held her for only a short while. Then we were told our beautiful little baby needed to be taken for an autopsy. At that moment, I realized she could not stay with us. The tears flowed, and I was a mess!

We left the hospital without our little baby the same afternoon. We went home to cry. We went home to sleep and not want to wake up.

Looking back, I wish I had taken photos with her that day and stayed with her longer. All I have are memories and feelings of sadness which will stay with me forever. Charlize became an angel on the 25th of June, just one day before my grandfather passed away five years earlier and born the day after. I am sure he was looking after her and watching over me.

We started preparing her funeral the day after. This was not something we'd thought about. We didn't know what she would wear, what her coffin would look like, what flowers we should have, what music we should play. Nothing. But we had a few days to think about it.

We bought her a pink teddy bear blanket to keep her warm. Then we chose beautiful music for her service, a white coffin, and white and pink flowers.

These were not meant to be a choice. Choosing to have a funeral was not in our plans for her.

Her funeral was held 3 July 2008. I was sick to my stomach and so anxious to hold my baby in my arms for the last time and say goodbye. My husband and I and a few family members sat in a small room of the chapel, and we held and cuddled her for as long as we could. We put a little dress over her that was given to us and then covered her with our pink teddy bear blanket. I was heartbroken. I took a few photos of her—but only one with me holding her.

After a beautiful but emotional service, we left the chapel and gathered at the cemetery where Charlize was to be buried. We each placed a pink rose on her coffin. I cried uncontrollably. Then, in a matter of moments, she was gone.

The days that followed were filled with tears. Every time I thought about my little Charlize, I would cry, knowing that I would never be able to hold her, kiss her, or feed her like I should have.

I was broken and felt no one understood my grief. Instead of feeling so down all day, I decided I needed to do something to keep myself busy. So I got out a pen and some paper and started writing. It was the only thing I knew I could do to keep me occupied while still remembering my baby, acknowledging she was part of our life. That book is a memory album filled with gifts we received, photos, and her story.

For many months I grieved, and to this day, I continually think of her, wondering what our lives would have been with her a part of it.

Six weeks after her birth, we were given the results of Charlize's autopsy. They found blood clots in her brain, and she was undernourished.

But my pregnancy story didn't end there. I miscarried again about nine months later and it broke my heart. I felt like a failure. Determined to have another baby, I fell pregnant again.

Throughout this pregnancy, I was injecting myself daily with Clexane, which is a medication to assist with blood clotting. I was worried everyday that something would happen and hoped my baby would be healthy.

On 23 July 2010, after an induction and an emergency cesarean, I gave birth to Damien, our rainbow baby. He was thirty-eight weeks and four days at birth. He was distressed from the umbilical cord wrapped around his neck, but this birth had a happy ending.

As I met him for the first time, a rush of pure love ran through my body. A feeling I've never felt before. That day as we sat together holding him, we sang to him and cried. Finally, we had our family. He is our little miracle.

During this time, I decided to write a blog about my losses as well as my new baby. I created charity auctions and donated the money to organizations that help support families with premature babies and loss.
When Damien was eighteen months old, I hit another roadblock when I suddenly had a seizure at work. I was diagnosed with epilepsy; causing pressure on my life as a mother and my ability to drive myself around just to go shopping with my baby by myself became a task on its own. I became

dependent on others, and often feeling the loss of freedom and a burden to my family. I was prescribed life-long medication which could risk future pregnancies.

In 2011, I again fell pregnant and again I miscarried after eight weeks. It was a stab in the heart, and again we were left disappointed and heartbroken. I was an emotional wreck! I could not deal with my grief and care for a young child. We took it easy and went away for a couple of days.

In January 2013, I fell pregnant with my little Ethan. During the pregnancy, I was again required to have Clexane injections daily and I started the pregnancy with progesterone to facilitate the growth of the embryo.

Due to low amniotic fluid, at thirty-eight weeks and four days, I was given the option to have another cesarean, have some testing done, or wait over the weekend to see if I would go into labour naturally. I decided on the caesarian so I wouldn't risk my baby's life. Ethan was born the exact same day I'd miscarried a year earlier—27 September 2013. I truly believe my angels were with me.

When my youngest was about nine months, I decided I'd write a memoir of my losses. *My Life of Loss* was published in March 2014.

This book changed everything for me. I was known in my local paper and I was picked up by a journalist from one of the country's largest selling women's magazine! Then, I was asked to be a guest speaker at a charity event for an organization that made beautiful angel gowns: Angel Gowns Australia, for babies that left us too soon. I was now in a pregnancy loss community. I needed to help people. My book did this without me even knowing it.

It was at that moment I knew other people wanted to be heard and share their stories of pregnancy too. So I found a group of people that wanted to write about their pregnancies. With them, I created a book of memoirs written by parents that had pregnancy or infant loss, IVF treatment or premature births.

This was when *Comfort for the tears, Light for the way* was published and brought into the world.

Two years on, I have grown a following with contacts all over the world. I was ready to create a new version of this book. More parents to help write their own story so they can help others in the same situation. This new book is *Comfort for the Tears*, a book of heartbreaking and heartwarming memoirs of pregnancy.

My experience through pregnancy loss and having beautiful, healthy babies has fulfilled my life and given me love, joy, and happiness. They have given me the courage and ability to continue to help people share their stories so they too can empower and help those that also need a shoulder to lean on.

Melissa Desveaux

Melissa is a mother of two boys and four angels.

Her struggles with pregnancy turned into hope when she realized there was a need for parents to be supported through pregnancy loss. She decided to write a memoir which lead to the opportunity to share her message to parents that they are not alone in their grief and they can be supported.

In 2014, Melissa decided to compile a book of memoirs called *Comfort for the Tears, Light for the way* to help parents write their own stories to heal and share their stories to help empower, inspire and heal others. This book was published and released in October 2016.

Melissa has dedicated her time encouraging people write their own personal stories, helping them publish their own book. *Comfort for the Tears* was compiled and published by Melissa as another way to give an opportunity to more parents to write about their babies and help to bring an understanding and awareness of pregnancy loss.

First Words
Written By My Husband In 2014

I am the proud father of two beautiful boys and an amazing wife, but what some of you may not know is that the journey my wife and I had to take to get to where we are today wasn't an easy one.

Our boys were two out of the six babies that we are grateful to have had. Many couples struggle to have kids and give up hope when it fails.

These issues are usually kept behind closed doors unless you have to have a funeral for a baby you've only held in your hands for a minute. From a male's perspective, it was very hard and challenging to go through all the ups and downs of the process.

I had to keep strong and try not to show my disappointment, pain, and agony during these setbacks. Seeing our attempts fail and my partner at the worst point in her life didn't help either, but together we managed to find the path to where we are today.

I don't think a man can ever understand what a woman goes through at this stage of their life, and I don't think any man can hold together as much as my wife did through these tough times. I am proud to say that my wife has finally written a book about the experiences we had together in her book titled My Life of Loss.

The original idea of the book was as a dedication to the babies we lost, and a celebration of the boys that we have. We realized that even though it is our story, it's a story that many people may be able to relate to, and also share with others that may be going through these tough times.

I believe that everyone has a story to tell; you don't have to be an accomplished author to tell your story. As long as there are people willing to read or listen to your story, your job has been done. Be thankful for the friends and family you have around you and never take your children for granted.

Jean-Francois Desveaux

Zak
A letter to Angel Gowns Australia

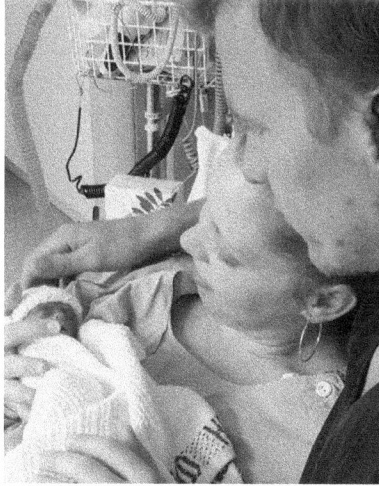

I was recently a recipient of one of your beautiful wraps for my baby that was born at twenty-two weeks & three days. I wanted to share my story with you and my heartfelt thank you for what you do.

My story is long, so I apologise in advance. But please know that what you did for me, my partner, and my baby will never be forgotten.

Every part of me feels that I need to write this for me, for Zak, for our families, for any of Zak's brothers and sisters that may come, for even one other person that this may help. In knowing that, it's impossible to know when or how to start.

It's been just over one month since he was born; a little longer than we knew what we were facing. I could say it was the day our world changed forever, but there have been so many of those days. My world changed so many times because

Poppyseed was my world.

It was 29 December that my first world change. Shane and I were on our way somewhere and that week.

I had taken so many pregnancy tests it was ridiculous! I remember each time, telling Shane I was barren; I was never going to be pregnant. Each time he would laugh at me and tell me it had only been a few months! Being pregnant, being a mum—that was it, that was all I ever wanted to be, and I never knew with more certainty that I wanted to be a mummy to Shane's babies. I wanted to give Shane a baby that he could tuck in every night and spoil every day, that would know that Daddy adored them and would adore Daddy. Because that's what Shane deserved.

So on that day, I took another one—and this time there was a line! So faint, but definitely a line. This was the first thing I learnt: positive tests don't come with two dark lines! I went into the kitchen and messaged Shane who was waiting outside in the car—he needed to come back upstairs. I told him I thought it was positive but it was so faint. We stared at it. We needed to know for sure, so we went straight to the shops and bought a digital one. No interpreting lines; it would be a yes or no!

I took the test and put it on the bench. The little clock icon flashed for an eternity. I walked away; Shane stood staring at it. And then my world changed. "It says yes!" he said. That was it; Poppyseed was on the way. I kissed Shane and then all the thoughts of what our baby was going to look like, all the things we would do together as a family and the images of being a mum rushed through my mind. That moment was so precious.

The next months were uneventful. Poppyseed was perfect. No morning sickness. No symptoms. Just this beautiful feeling of growing our baby. I know for sure that I felt Poppyseed move at eleven weeks—pure love. I spent every moment from then focusing on feeling our baby.

At twelve weeks, we had our first photoshoot. Our baby was real and was incredible. Poppyseed was a wriggler! After some photos, I asked if I could hear our baby. That sound ... it's like nothing I had ever heard before. Strong, steady, calming.

Again, weeks went by uneventfully. We were in our second trimester now and of course, that meant we were out of the danger stage. This was lesson number two: when you are pregnant, you are never out of the danger stage. Everyone and anyone could now know that we were having a perfect little baby! I would have shouted it from the rooftops if I could have, but I settled with telling everyone I knew. I planned maternity leave, daycare, swim school, and the nursery. Poppyseed would have it all.

I loved being pregnant, loved it. I slept like a trooper and napped most days. I went off meat and had to often bargain with Shane on a suitable amount of meat that I would eat at dinner time. I would have my hand on my belly all the time, sometimes just to try and feel Poppyseed; other times to say, "Hey baby, I know you are in there and I love you."

Daddy would talk to Poppyseed too. Those moments, when I think back, still make me smile and bring tears. Daddy would tell Poppyseed all the things they were going to do together, would tell Poppyseed to be good and to look after me. Daddy even sang to Poppyseed. It was the three of us and we were just living the most perfect life.

Time grew closer to find out the sex. Anyone that knows me knows I'm a planner. There wasn't a chance I was leaving that appointment without knowing whether our baby was a girl or a boy. As we grew closer, the suspense was overwhelming and the days were so long. I swore all along it was a girl and Shane agreed. Girls are everywhere in both our families and we were going to be hard-pressed to change this.

About a week before, I remember a clear feeling that Poppyseed was a boy. And I was so sorry for all those months I had called him a girl and for his pretty girly nickname!! Daddy wasn't convinced.

April 20 came. We went to our appointment and again saw beautiful pictures of our baby. Poppyseed was unstoppable with wiggles. So many photos and measurements were taken. There was a strong, beautiful heartbeat. And then we asked—I think I saw it before Alison (our sonographer) said, "Let me show you." Poppyseed was a boy!

I had no idea what I was going to do with a boy, but I could not have been happier. I still remember Shane's words: "I can make boys!" I had my two boys and in that moment, I could not have loved them anymore. That was the happiest moment of my life; another day my world changed.

We made everyone wait. I wanted to photograph our reveal and my beautiful photographer was on the way to our house that night. Shane wasn't so keen, but I remember saying, "This might be the only bubby we have and I will regret it if I don't have these photos." Only now, I realise how profound that was, and how much those photos now mean to me: the smiles, the happiness, and the love that can be seen in those photos I will cherish forever.

While we waited, I was in a daze. We were going to have a baby boy! Shane would have to do the toilet training because, you know, he had the equipment! I was going to dress him in suspenders and all kinds of adorable boys' clothes, and his dad was going to save him from this. Shane looked up AFL onesies; our baby was going to love AFL, just like his dad. That's exactly why the very first toy Poppyseed ever had was the football, bought as soon as we knew our baby was on the way.

That night, we took pictures and shared the news with our family and friends. Poppyseed was a boy! I fell asleep that night with a smile on my face. My two boys … the world was just as it should be.

The next lesson was the hardest—the fall, from the highest of highs to the absolutely lowest of lows. Without knowing, that very next day was another day my world changed.

My phone rang while I was at work. It was the doctor's surgery, telling me my doctor wanted me to come in and the earliest appointment they had was just after 1pm. Everyone knows that's not good. Shane and I convinced ourselves that it was related to the position of my placenta and because of that, I went to the appointment alone. The first one I ever did or would do without Shane.

When I arrived, our wonderful doctor took me straight in— another bad sign—you don't ever NOT wait for the doctor. He began to tell me that something was abnormal with bub- by's brain. "I can't tell you much, we need another scan, it will be okay, we will get the scan done and go from there." I had only heard the first line. I called Shane while I was walking to my car. Holding the report in my hand, I tried to explain through tears while trying to breathe.

I sent him the report with the big words and we began Googling. Somehow, we managed to convince ourselves it was common and it was all going to be cleared up at the next scan. Of course it was.

That weekend was a long weekend. It meant an extra painful day until the next scan. It consumed my every thought at that point and all of me willed for it to be okay. I'd give anything; I'd do anything to make my little boy okay.

April 26th came and we arrived at the second level ultra- sound. Our specialist started measuring: perfect arms, perfect legs, perfect fingers, perfect toes, perfect hands, perfect eyes, nose, face; perfect. It wasn't possible for anything to be wrong when he was so perfect in every other way. Poppy-seed was especially cheeky today—he would continue to flip when she walked away to confuse her. He hid his left ankle and then shortly after would only show his left ankle. To this day, these remain some of our best memories of our little boy and his cheeky personality.

Then she said, "I can see what they were looking at in his brain." My heart broke again; this wasn't going to be the outcome we had convinced ourselves of. We were led into a consultation room, big words were said, pictures were drawn, and the world just became a blur. Nothing made sense and there were no answers. "We need to do an MRI," she told us. This meant more waiting and days of despair. I think I knew then that this wasn't going to be the happy ending I'd so badly wanted.

That night, I told Shane I was going to have a shower. He was going to call his mum and I thought he would be busy and I could be loud in the shower and not worry him. I sat in the bottom of the shower and I just cried. A moment later, there was Shane, fully clothed in the shower holding me. Shane and I spoke about the choice we might have to make, but in the end, there was no choice. I knew I would rather live a lifetime in pain than have my baby go through a moment of it. I'm so truly grateful that Shane and I were always on the same page, often without words.

I don't quite remember where it fits in the story, but I remember one night finding a story so similar to ours (although I didn't know this at the time). It was written by a lady outlining what she had experienced. Hers was much shorter than mine! As I read it, I cried; it was only reading her story that it hit me. If this was bad, I was going to have to go through labour. Now I'm a smart person, but for the life of me I had no idea why I didn't realise this earlier. I turned to Shane and tried to tell him what I had just realised. I said, "If this is bad, I'm going to have to..." I couldn't finish. He said, "...give birth. I know, baby." He had already realised this.

Shane didn't think reading was a good idea, but I know that it was. It was because of that story that I got through. That story gave me the steps of what I was going to endure. I knew before every step what was going to come next. I will be forever grateful to that woman for sharing her story.

April 29 came, the day of our MRI. It was a Friday, and we had already been told that any scans wouldn't be looked at until the specialist came to the hospital on Tuesday. Another impossible wait. As I lay there in the machine with my headphones on, I thought, "Where are Poppyseed's headphones?" I kept saying to myself—hoping it meant Poppyseed heard it—"It's okay baby, don't be scared baby, I love you," over and over again.

Shane and I drove home. Drives to and from the hospital were mostly silent now, just lost in our thoughts. Shane went to work and I went to bed. Then my phone rang; it was our specialist. She told me that we needed to come back straight away. She said the scans were "bad, really bad," and they didn't need to wait until Tuesday to review them.
"

I rang Shane and he came straight home. I was talking to my family, updating them and I remember hearing Shane cry. I had never seen or heard this incredible man break like that and I rushed off the phone to comfort him. Shane and I'd managed so far to take it in turns. On the days that he struggled, I was strong and on the far more frequent days I struggled, he was strong.
We made the silent drive to the hospital again. This was the point at which we became "famous" at the hospital. No more waiting rooms, no more explaining our story; we said my name and we were immediately ushered through. I remember joking that it must be really bad. I joked a lot—I still do

because it helps.

The midwife told us our baby's brain was "wild." That was the word she used—"wild." Then our specialist came in and asked if we would like to see the scan. Of course I did. I needed to know what everyone was looking at; I needed to see, to understand. She explained that where bubby's brain should be had significantly degraded and bubby had very little grey matter remaining. A "catastrophic insult" was what she called it. None of that made sense.

I was healthy; I had taken my pregnancy vitamins, I had not eaten anything I wasn't supposed to. I had done it all "right." Stats like one in one hundred thousand were discussed; stories like only ever seeing it one other time in a young girl who was in a horrific car accident—still none of it made sense.

The outcome for our Poppyseed was horrific: seizures, disability, no intellect, unknown impact on his physical abilities. She said, "Do you need time to talk about it?" Shane and I looked at each other, and at the same time, we said we didn't. That's one of the things I'm grateful for in this whole thing. For me, there was no choice; the choice was made for us.

What followed was paperwork to sign, appointments made, more paperwork. Questions about whether we wanted photos, handprints, footprints. I just wanted my baby. I signed everything, completely in a daze. There would be a birth certificate, we were told, and a death certificate. We would have to arrange a funeral. For any birth over twenty weeks, this is a legal requirement. This was all new learnings for us. We had one question: would our baby be born alive? "We don't know," was the answer. "Possibly, possibly not, but if he is, it wouldn't be for long."

The social worker came in. As a social worker myself, that was always going to be interesting. She told me I needed to take my "social work" hat off and put my "mum" hat on. I remember thinking—and later told Shane—I can't do that. My "social work" hat was the only thing keeping me in that room, processing and understanding the choices I was making. Without that hat, the mum in me would have fallen apart.

After being told about payments we would be entitled to and what seemed like a lot of talking without taking a breath, we were allowed to go home. I was still carrying and feeling my baby, but I knew that I had just signed his little life away. I just kept telling him that I was sorry, telling him I loved him.

Shane said to me a few days, maybe weeks, later, "That was the day we lost our son." That was the day he was taken from us. And he is right. What came next were just steps along the way.

That day I cried. I felt guilty and felt hopeless. But the next day, I decided that my baby was not going to spend the last few days feeling nothing but my despair. He didn't deserve that. He had done nothing wrong. He made us the happiest we had ever been. So we went about having a beautiful weekend together, just the three of us. Of course we were destroyed and heartbroken, but we did our best to talk to him, to laugh about him, to make him have his last few days as happy ones. I was helpless, but I could do that for him. On Sunday, we went in to start the medication. This was just a quick trip in, take the meds, monitor for an hour, and then go home again. It was relatively uneventful. At the time the tablet was handed to me, I burst into tears. I knew as soon as I took this it was over, it was real. The nurse began to cry as well. Immediately I felt guilty! But she held my hand, said some beautiful words and after the hour asked if she could hug me as I left. I could never turn down a hug.

The next day was Labour Day. Ironic, I know. After hours and several calls to the birth suite, at 3:30pm we were told to come in. They had tried to bring us in when it was quiet and put us in a room semi out of the way; all these things they had to consider for us. We got to the hospital, my family and Shane's parents.

Shane and I were led to the room we would be in. There was a butterfly on the door. This seemed to confuse the reception lady and she doubled checked with the midwife that we were supposed to be in that room. When she left, I asked the midwife if the butterfly meant something. "Yes," she said, "it's our subtle way of saying what's going on in the room."

"Not very subtle!" I laughed. And later, I reflected that I didn't know if I should be insulted. At five and a half months, that poor lady thought I was full term! Too many cakes and sweets that were blamed on Poppyseed!

The Friday before, the day we signed away our baby, we were told the process. The medication on Saturday would ensure that it would be quick; in the time that they had followed this procedure no one had gone over forty-eight hours. We would be admitted and then they would start two tablets every four hours for five rounds. After a twelve-hour break, it was the same process. That should be it. Okay, my "social work" hat understood that.

So we went through the first round, again uneventful; nothing happened.

During this time, every midwife was beautiful; everyone one of them reassured me, cared for us both and made me feel like I was in capable hands. We were asked to pick a beautiful hand-sewn blanket that Poppyseed could be wrapped in, that we could then keep. Daddy chose one with cars on it, but he had bonded with one midwife over AFL, so she chose one with soccer balls on it and told us to have both. She showed us the beautiful hand-sewn wrap that Poppyseed would be placed in; this too we could keep. It was made from donated wedding dresses by a foundation called Angel Gowns Australia—who knew these wonderful people existed? We were shown the little beanie and the tiny booties that he would be dressed in.

We were shown the beautiful memory box we would go home with. Families that had experienced what we were going through donated these. Ours had a little girl's name on it and we agreed instantly that one day we would do this for Poppyseed too. We were told that professional photographers would come after the birth and take photos for us; anything we wanted, anything we needed.

Of course we wanted nothing but to take our baby home, but there's no doubt that the amazing memories that we received, the love and care that was paid, and the time we had together that was captured helped ease some of that pain.

After the first twelve-hour break, we went again, medication every four hours, five rounds—and again nothing. With everything that had happened to us, of course I was going to break this record too. Then the review came, and a suggestion that I was going to be sent home before starting the whole process again from the beginning. I refused. I was not going home; I was not leaving. I didn't want a rest.

Luckily for me, the specialist stepped in and told the doctors to give me another one of the tablets I took on Sunday and go again. This time, the number of tablets in the four-hour rounds was doubled. The outcome for Poppyseed was known; now it was time to get me through it. I apologised to her for ruining her forty-eight-hour stat; we laughed.

So we went again—another tablet and another round. Slowly things started to happen. Very slowly. A side effect of the tablets is high temp, so I spent a twelve hour period with a temperature of thirty-nine point five. I had constant blood tests to make sure I hadn't contracted an infection. I had smashed their forty-eight-hour time frame.

Another twelve-hour rest and the fourth round was started. Finally, things started to move. Contractions started coming and we just had to wait for my cervix to get to five centimeters so my water could be broken. After that happened, it would go quick, they told me. I didn't believe them.

At one point the pain was so excruciating I said to Shane, "I can't do this, I want to go home." He just rubbed my back, gave me my ten thousandth jug of ice and told me I could. They asked me if I wanted an epidural. I said no. I had all my choices and all my control taken away from me; I was about to lose my baby—but I had this choice, I could decide this and I had control. I settled for morphine and gas.

It kept running through my head: Tara, your baby is going to be tiny; Tara, your baby is not going to be alive; Tara, you will have to say goodbye; Tara, you won't get to take your baby home. Over and over as if trying to convince myself; trying to prepare myself.

My waters were finally broken, and they were right; things moved quickly, or maybe they didn't. Shane would have to answer that because what comes next is hazy for me at best.

I asked Shane, with extreme pressure below and the desire to push, "How will I know when I should?" Shane asked the midwife. "She will know," she said. I didn't. I had never done this before. I had no idea what I was doing.

A point came when I just couldn't help but push and with one, Shane told me he could see his head. The midwife told me he was coming and with just one more push he would be here. Again my mantra, a final push and I knew he was here because the relief was instant; no more pain.

At 1:40pm on 5 May, Zak, our beautiful baby was born at twenty-two weeks and three days. He never took a breath. He never opened his eyes. And most importantly, he never had a second of pain. Daddy cut his umbilical cord and he was handed to me.

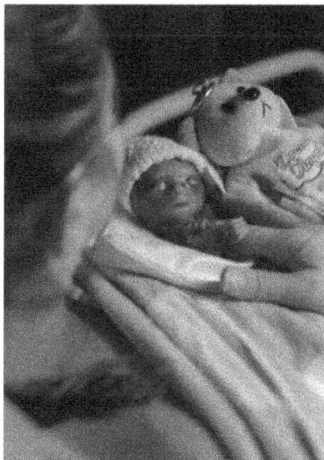

"He is perfect," he said, "he is absolutely perfect." And he was. I don't know why, (probably due to drugs!) but at that point, I was calm, the physical pain was over, we had done what we needed to do. I was holding my baby. Shane was overcome and cried. I held him and told him it was okay.

I later found out the midwife that delivered Zak had her own experiences at twenty-two weeks and twenty-seven weeks. I had so much admiration for this woman, to keep doing what she does. But I was so glad she was there; she really knew how I was feeling, she really understood. She laughed when we laughed, she joked when we did, she cried when we cried (when he was born), she was angry when we were angry. She said all the things I needed to hear as a woman who had just become a mother. She knew and I'm forever grateful.

I held him. I looked at him, trying to take in every detail, trying to figure out his features. He had my face—round—and my eyes—big and round. That was where I ended. He had his daddy's nose and lips; he had his daddy's long lean body type. He had perfect fingers and toes, long legs, and massive feet. He had perfect little ears and fingernails and toenails. He was beautiful.

Our families came in; I was never going to force anyone, but he was there for cuddles if they wanted. All of them did. We have photos and we cherish these. He felt all of their love.

I wasn't done quite yet though. It became apparent a while later that I must have retained some placenta and surgery would be required to stop my constant bleeding. It was estimated at a minimum I had lost approximately one point three litres. And after a quick faint in the shower, I was rushed into emergency surgery. I had forms to sign, consent for a hysterectomy, acknowledging that I may die. I was wheeled out, looking at Shane holding Zak and I thought, This is it, he is going to lose his son and me in the same night and I couldn't bear to think about what that would do to him. I told Shane I loved him as tears ran down my face, and I told him to look after our son.

As they put me to sleep, my calmness left me, and I burst into tears. I don't know who she was, but at that point a lady reached down grabbed my hand and told me I was going to be okay. That was the last thing I remembered.

I woke up and was wheeled back to Shane and Zak. Shane later told me that about two and a half hours had passed. I had missed Zak's bath because the photographers couldn't wait, but they had plenty of photos of it for me. We have since received the professional photos and there are some truly beautiful ones of me holding my son and of the three of us together. Thankfully we have these photos because my memory of these being taken is non-existent. I don't remember it at all. Shane says they wheeled me back and instantly began taking photos. They did a wonderful job.
There are photos of Shane and Zak, and in hindsight, I'm so glad he got that time with his son, just the two of them. I had so much time with Poppyseed; just him and me, and I'm glad

they got their time too.

Shane and I decided early on that we didn't want to prolong our time with Zak. We wanted to remember him being perfect and we knew that as time went on this would affect his little body. Although it wasn't part of the plan, we soon both agreed to have him overnight with us. He was placed in a special crib with a cool pad on the bottom. He couldn't be beside me because the crib required constant power, but from my bed, I could see him wrapped in his wrap on his blanket and I could feel him with us.

In the morning, we said our goodbyes. We were both scared to lift him, but at the last moment, I asked the midwife to lift him. I wanted to kiss him one more time. We were told Zak could be brought back to us at any time, that he wouldn't leave the ward until we left the hospital. But we knew that was the last time we would see him.

Zak went with so many things: his football of course, his two jumpsuits—one saying "I love Mummy," the other "I love Daddy"—and matching socks, three blankets—one from Mummy, one knitted by Grandma, and one brought by Nani (wherever he was going he was going to be warm!)—a teddy from Nani, and a teddy from his three cousins that he would never meet but loved him dearly. He went with Mummy's T-shirt that had Daddy's blue handprints on from his gender reveal. He went with the bracelet that Daddy had made for Mummy. He went with all the love that his mum and dad had for each other and for him.

After several more days and a late night medical emergency call, I had decided I was ready to go home. It had almost been a week in hospital and I was being wakened for constant monitoring, including a standing heart rate every hour, even throughout the night. I asked the nurse what I had to do to go home. She gave me a list, and within twenty-four hours, I had checked this list off.

Mother's Day arrived. I was going home; I had had enough. We waited patiently for the doctor and at 3pm, she arrived. I was signed off and the next step was here—to leave the hospital without my baby. Instead of my baby, I had flowers in my hand and I was wheeled out to the pick-up bay. I again told Zak I was sorry and I loved him. As Shane drove us home, tears ran down my face.

The next few days were a blur. We arranged the funeral and it was as beautiful as it could be. There were moments that were just so surreal. Questions that we never thought we would have to answer. And from then until now, we take it a day at a time.

There are moments that I'm overwhelmed with emotions, like the day his birth certificate arrived, or the one where his room decals came, or the one where I opened his death certificate, with the cause of death listed as "Open Lip Bilateral Schizencephaly." But I am comforted by words that were said at Zak's funeral. Even if we knew why, even if there were answers, this wouldn't take away our pain and this wouldn't make it any easier.

I am incredibly firm in my belief that it is my job to be strong for my son. I am his mum and that's my job. And more than anything, I am adamant that my son will not be remembered with just tears and heartbreak. He brought us so much joy, so much happiness and he deserves for his memory to bring us laughter and smiles. That's something else I can do for him.

People have struggled to know how to help, to know how to respond. This I understand. But in response to this I say: for the short moment it is hard to say anything, it is a million times harder for us to breathe or to function. I want my son acknowledged; I want to talk about him, for the world to realise he existed. For his memory to be strong; anything else to me is just not acceptable. There is nothing anyone can say to make it better and there's nothing anyone can ask me that I haven't already answered, so there's no fear of upsetting me. If all else fails, just a hug, an "I'm sorry for your loss" — that's all that is needed and it truly means the world.

To Zak, my beautiful baby boy ... I will love you for a lifetime, every day. I now have no fear of my time ending, because that will be the day I see you again. Until then, I will miss you every day. I am so sorry I couldn't help you, but I hope you hear me every night when I go to sleep and see me every morning when I place your blanket on Daddy's and my pillow. You will always be my first baby and you will never be forgotten.

To Shane, there are no words to thank you. You are my strength every day; you are the reason I'm breathing. You are my everything. I'm so sorry you had to go through this pain, but I will spend my lifetime making all your dreams come true like you do for me.
To the midwives at RBWH, thank you for all your love and care, for Shane and me and but mostly for our Zak. You are truly amazing people and what you did for us made the impossible bearable. I will remember each of you forever.

To Angel Gowns Australia, thank you for existing. Thank you for giving us something beautiful to put our baby in and dressing him so beautifully. I will be grateful for that forever.

To Precious Wings, thank you for our memory box. Thank you for filling my hands with something to take home and for giving us precious memories to remember our baby. To the beautiful family who lost their baby and dedicated their box, thank you—we know your pain and your gift eased ours. We too will buy a box in memory of Zak one day.

To Heartfelt, the incredible photographers that came that night, the day our photos arrived was a happy one. Thank you, without you I would not have memories of my baby's first bath or pictures of my boys together. What you have given us is priceless.

To our family and friends, thank you is not enough; we will never be able to repay the love and care you have given us. Thank you for loving me, and thank you even more for loving my son.

To any other mother that goes through anything like this, I know your pain. I've felt it. It does lift and you are not alone. You are strong, stronger than you ever thought you would need to be—stronger than anyone should ever have to be. Just breathe. I promise it gets easier.

While it seemed inconceivable at the time; two and a half years have passed. Zak has had two birthdays, which of course included cake! Zak is and always will be our son; he is remembered with love and celebrated always and each year we figure out how to do that better and louder. And we now share his celebrations with his little sister, Ava. The two of them together are pure love and these moments give us comfort for the tears.

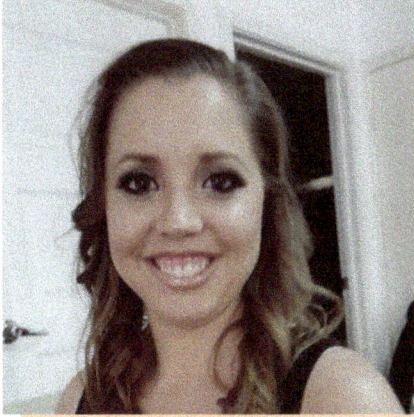

Tara Watson

Tara Watson (Roulston), Contributor to Comfort for the Tears, is a mother to Zak, Ava, and a proud step-mum to Sienna and Elle. Tara is a Social Worker and has spent her professional career in the field of Child Protection.

Tara wrote the story of Zak after he was stillborn at twenty-two weeks because the thought of the world not knowing him was too painful to endure. However, unexpectedly, Zak's story has since gone on to provide comfort to others. Each year, Zak's family is able to share his story and his memory with a louder voice.

Their hope is that by breaking down the stigma and silence of baby loss, they can make it a little bit easier and less lonely for the families that will inevitably travel this path.

Our Journey to Happiness

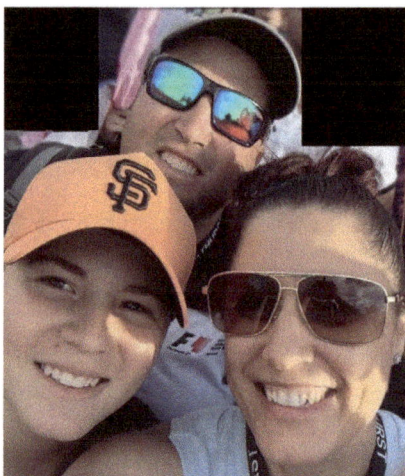

I was just nineteen-years-old in 1999 when I married Kevin, and the furthest thing from my mind was not being able to get pregnant. Our goal was a honeymoon baby—it never occurred to us that it wouldn't happen. Our honeymoon lasted for six weeks; we had all the time in the world. I had never been on the pill, we were both young and healthy, and wasn't this what I'd always planned?

When we arrived back home, I was not pregnant. Two periods had been and gone since being married and I was thinking, Wow, how can I not be pregnant?

We tried for one whole year and by this time I was getting quite concerned that I was not falling pregnant. So I went to my GP, who told me I was young, don't stress, and keep trying. Well, that didn't sit well with Kevin and me, as we really wanted to start a family.

Over the next few months, I did lots of research and asked

other ladies what they did when they had trouble getting pregnant. A lot of women had used an ovulation tester, so I started to check my temperature and doing the whole wee-on-the-stick thing to find out when I was ovulating. Through-out the months, I tried this but my hormone levels stayed the same. I began to really fear that getting pregnant was not going to be possible for me, so I headed straight back to the doctors.

This time I was taken seriously and referred to a gynecologist, Dr. Lovell. But it took nine weeks to get an appointment with Dr. Lovell, a process which left me feeling upset and confused. Eventually, we got to see Dr. Lovell. She was sweet and talked softly but firmly. She told me, "We need to do further testing on both you and your husband so we can sort this out."

We left that office with a stack of paperwork. The lovely receptionist booked us for another appointment in three weeks.

The next few weeks were busy. At that time, I owned a hair and beauty salon, and we were in peak season. I loved my job, loved managing my business and my staff. But behind that was an immense weight of worry about our results. I had blood tests and scans booked, and Kevin had to do a series of sperm count tests.

When we went back to the doctor's, it was hard to sit in the waiting room surrounded by pregnant women. I just wanted to scream!

Dr. Lovell did not have good news for us. I had polycystic ovaries and a blockage in my left tube and my left ovary had cysts all over it. She then said, "I am really sorry to tell you, but Kevin has a low sperm count." It felt like a bullet had just gone through my heart. Kevin said to me, "I am sorry, honey." But I replied, "Don't be sorry—it's you and me."

I don't remember much else of what Dr. Lovell said, but she did advise us to look into IVF. The next few weeks were hard, and I cried a lot. I kept asking, "Why me?" Kevin was amazing support. He would lie with me and let me cry, and he would always know the right things to say.

We had to wait three months for our appointment at IVF Australia. It felt like all we did was wait and worry. During this time, I turned twenty-one and it felt like time was ticking. All around me, friends and family were getting pregnant. Each time I heard the news, my heart would break a little more but the words that followed would be, "Congrats, that's great news." As we had kept our pregnancy struggles to ourselves, keeping a straight face was getting harder and harder.

Yippee!! The day for our IVF appointment arrived and I was more excited than Christmas. We arrived at the clinic, and again we were bombarded with paperwork—the questions were so in-depth and personal. The walls of the clinic were covered in people's success stories and beautiful baby photos. I sat there and read some of them and, for the first time since this journey began, hope started to creep in.

Dr. Joel Bernstein talked to us about the process and as I had problems and Kevin had problems. The type of IVF process required for us would be the latest technique called ICSI. The process involved the collection of my eggs and the collection of Kevin's sperm. The sperm was inserted directly in the egg so that the hardest job was done and all that needed to happen was the fertilisation process. The doctor then proceeded to fill out our paperwork so we could start the cycle. Our bloods were taken by the nurse and we were given a chart to follow and an instruction book. Our nurse was wonderful; so understanding and calm.

We left with an overload of information and the instructions to "live by your phone" as the nurse would call us about our results. The nurse called to tell us that we needed to let the clinic know when my period started. More waiting—by now I loved waiting! Day one of my period arrived and the nurse told me I needed to come in for blood tests starting on day five of my period. For seven days in a row, I had blood taken and on the seventh day, the nurse told me that things were looking positive. She handed me a bag containing my hormone injections, pessaries, and other tablets. She outlined how to use them and guided me through the upcoming procedure.

Every day for six weeks, at 6pm, I self-administered the hormone treatment. Our lives now revolved around hormone injections and doctor's appointments. I became so focused on this treatment. I put all my energy, prayers, and emotion into trying to stay confident and positive each day.

The injections made me bloat up and my tummy was so sore and bruised. But finally we were given some good news. The nurse said, "Your eggs are looking good, nice and full, and lots of follicles there." I was booked into day-surgery for egg collection. We talked that night about the next chapter in our lives and the thought of finally getting pregnant, and I was so excited!

On egg collection day, I was so nervous, but Kevin reassured me and kept me confident. While I had my eggs harvested, Kevin was in the next room collecting sperm so the cross-match could be done. When I woke up, I was told twelve eggs had been collected. The scientist, Renee, came out to tell us that the cross matching had also been done. So now we had to go home and wait for the results. It was a funny mixture of feelings: happy, sad, worried, relieved, concerned, and most of all excited that in a few days, those embryos would be implanted.

The next day, Renee phoned to tell us that of the twelve, only six had continued to split and divide; so only six viable embryos. That was a hard blow. All those injections, a day of surgery, all the discomfort … and I only had six left. The tears started flowing again, and I couldn't believe this was happening. Renee called the next day to tell us we needed to come into the clinic for an embryo transfer. The rest of the viable embryos would be frozen.

On transfer day, we were taken into a very cold, very sterile room to wait. Finally, the embryo transfer was done. We were told to carry on as normal, but to come back in fourteen days. If my period arrived, I was to call the clinic ASAP. What on earth is "normal" when you are continually racing to the bathroom to check if you have any spotting and every little pain or twitch makes you worry? It got so tense that every time I called Kevin, his first words would be, "Is everything okay?"

We made it to day fourteen. We arrived at the clinic at 6:30 am to be first in line to have bloods. We went straight through, and I was getting a little excited. But we were faced with a fresh slap in the face when, two hours after leaving the clinic, my period arrived. I looked down at my underwear in shock! I had made it to fourteen days and was beginning to hope what a cruel surprise. I could hear in Kevin's voice how disappointed he was, but he replied, "It's okay, honey. It was the first try—we will go again."

I spent the whole morning in bed crying and feeling so let down. I wondered how did it not take; it was fertilized and it was in there.

A phone call from the clinic confirmed what I already knew—I wasn't pregnant. I then started thinking that maybe it's me; maybe I am not cut out to be pregnant, and maybe it's my body's way of telling me, "Don't go there." Kevin arrived home and he was so supportive. Not once did he say, "Don't worry," or "Get over it." Not once did he let me feel I was letting him down.

Five more times over a fourteen-month period we went through the process, and every time was a failure. By now, Kevin and I were drained physically, emotionally, and financially. My dream of having my own baby was slipping away. There were babies being born all around me and everywhere I looked were pregnant ladies. And then there was me, feeling angrier by the day.

By this time, all my embryos were used up, so the process for another egg collection began with another round of hormone injections and blood tests and the long drive down to the clinic, as well as running my successful business and keeping my personal life locked up so the world thought I was normal.

The time arrived for my next egg collection, but this time I hypostemulated, which meant my body went into overdrive and the follicles had over-produced, so they had to give me a drug to reverse it. So no eggs collected that day. Yet another effort that was all for nothing.

The next egg collection was successful and I got twenty-two eggs—wow! The doctor and scientist were really happy, and I was feeling well after this egg collection. I was referred to another specialist, Dr. David Knight who was studying and trying new techniques that I might benefit from. We met with Dr. Knight and immediately I felt I was in good hands. We returned to the clinic three days later for a fresh transfer. Hopes were high. The doctor was confident, and we were too.

During the transfer, the doctor noticed my uterus was tilted and that was why we were having so much trouble. He placed the embryo in a higher spot and said, "Let's give that a go."

Six days later, my period arrived. I sobbed to my mum, "I am not doing this anymore. You wouldn't do this to a dog. I am done." My mum was so strong and brave. She said, "You can do it and I will hold your hand the whole way." I agreed to go one more time; after that, I could say I did all I could. My mum came each day during that round, to all my blood tests and spoke with the doctor and nurses and kept my chin up. It was a relief for Kevin because I know he was tired from trying to keep me strong and he was hurting just as much as me.

The last round began in October 2003, a Monday morning and a public holiday. The staff was amazing, working any time that my body's hormones were ready. We entered the transfer room and everything was ready to go. The doctor gave me a booster to place under my bottom to boost me up and back at the right angle. On this transfer, we decided to have two embryos implanted. The transfer went smooth, and it was less painful and less invasive.

The doctor said, "Fingers crossed, and enjoy the rest of your day off."

I took this transfer with a very carefree attitude. I had already decided that the transfer was not going to work and that I was just going through the motions to say that I had tried my best. The next fourteen days were spent working long hours, taking my medication and living life.

Day fourteen arrived—again—and Mum and I went back to the clinic for the dreaded blood test. After a short wait, Anne, the nurse took me through. Anne's smile was always so comforting and warm. As she took my blood, she talked to me about staying positive and happy and enjoying the journey. I always put on a strong face, but inside I was a mess. The bloods were done and Anne said she would call me at 11am.

The car ride home was quiet. I think my mum had everything crossed and I believe that she had never prayed so much. But she always spoke so confident and calmly and always said the right things.

We arrived home and my mum stayed with me. We kept ourselves busy around the house making beds and hanging washing, and at exactly 11am, the home phone rang. It was Anne from the clinic. I put the phone on loudspeaker so Mum could hear, as I was not repeating any bad news. "Congratulations, you're pregnant," Anne said. I was silent for a while then responded with, "Are you sure?" She said, "Yes, your levels are very high. Keep an eye on things, and we need you to come down tomorrow morning for more bloods." I managed to stammer out a "Thank you" and hung up.

Well, the tears rolled again but this time they were tears of joy. My mum was excited and crying too. I then called Kevin, and before he could say hello I blurt out, "It bloody worked, we are having a baby!" He too was very emotional and happy and relieved. Next, I called my dad. After we'd said our hellos, he asked me why I was calling. I said, "Because you're going to be a Nunnu (Grandfather) again." There was silence on the other end. "Dad? Dad, are you okay?" He said, "Yes, I am just so happy. Thank God." I could hear the happiness in his voice. Kevin called his mum and she too was overjoyed.

The next day arrived and I had never been so eager to get to the clinic. My bloods were taken and an ultrasound was done. The doctor had some more news for us: we were expecting twins! For the first time in a long time I smiled, and it was a real smile.

At my next appointment a week later, Anne told me I was ready to see a gynecologist. "Are you sure?" I asked. She said, "I am more than sure, you are nearly six weeks pregnant and our job is done." As much as I had dreaded going to the clinic, it had become a safe place. But I called the gynecologist and made an appointment to see her when I reached eight weeks pregnant.

By week seven, I was vomiting all day, every day—but I didn't care. My days consisted of working and vomiting.

Eventually, the vomiting got so bad I was admitted to hospital. My gyno, Dr. Lovell, met me at the hospital in the maternity ward and checked me over. She put me straight onto an IV drip and ordered an ultrasound. I felt afraid again—nine months is such a long time when you have no control over what's happening. The ultrasound was done and during the scan, Dr. Lovell told me that Twin A was not doing as well as Twin B and she was a little concerned. She kept me in for five days and during that time, I was still vomiting but not as bad.

At this time, Kevin and I decided to sell the business and focus on the pregnancy. The shop sold in four weeks and I spent my time resting at home, still vomiting. I got up one morning and started doing some washing when all of a sudden I got cramps. Scared out of my skin, I called my mum as Kevin was too far away. Mum said she was on her way and told me to go lie down and not to move. As I lay down, I felt wet and realised I was bleeding. As soon as Mum arrived, she raced to call Dr. Lovell.

Mum took me back to hospital. I was stressing like no tomorrow. But Dr. Lovell greeted me calmly. She explained that I had a small tear and that the bleeding should slow down. I went straight down to ultrasound and there it was: two strong heartbeats. What an awesome sight. I remained in hospital for seven more days and given more IV fluids and full bed rest. At this stage, I was only eleven weeks.

Weeks eleven through sixteen were okay. I was still vomiting, and the only things I could eat were pizza and Pepsi, and very little of that. I visited Dr. Lovell at her clinic each Wednesday at 12:30 and she was happy with my progress. Each week she did a small ultrasound, and Twin A was always smaller than Twin B. Twin A was sitting very low and Twin B was sitting higher.

Week seventeen was a sad week. One morning, I woke to heavy bleeding. Kevin took me straight to the hospital.

Dr. Lovell examined me and did an ultrasound. She said, "Twin A is coming away. I am sorry, but this baby is not going to make it. However, Twin B is happy, so that's very important."

Dr. Lovell explained that I would have heavy bleeding, but I might not pass the baby as it could be absorbed and would pass through during labour. I bled for the remaining time of my pregnancy. I was so sad, and I worried for my baby I was still carrying. I worried about my baby I lost and never met. I had so many emotions.

I left hospital and continued my pregnancy journey. The weeks passed quickly and before we knew it, I was thirty-five weeks pregnant. My beautiful family gave me a surprise baby shower at my sister-in-law's house. Kevin had a hard time convincing me to get in the car. I kept saying, "I don't want to go visiting." He said, "You stay home all day, every day, and the only outing you have is to doctor's appointments!" I'm glad I listened to him because I had the best time and I am forever grateful to my family for that experience.

At thirty-nine weeks pregnant Dr, Lovell said to me, "I don't think I will be seeing you in my clinic for a check-up again, I think I will be seeing you in the labour ward." I was filled with excitement each day, wondering if today was the day.

My waters broke one Sunday morning in June. I felt so happy. I yelled out to Kevin, "Get up, get up! It's happening—my waters just broke!" I called my mum to tell her the news and ask her to meet us at the hospital.

By now, I was a regular at the maternity ward, so all the nurses were excited for me. I just couldn't wait to meet my baby. We still didn't know if we would be welcoming a boy or a girl. When we had the transfer done, I knew we had one girl and one boy embryo put in and through the whole process and all the ultrasounds, we never found out. It didn't matter to me. I was having a baby—woo-hoo!

I laboured for twenty-four long hours, and I had every pain relief offered to me. Kevin and Mum were there the whole time, as was Dr. Lovell. After seventeen hours, an epidural was ordered for me as I had stopped dilating. After receiving the epidural, my body relaxed and I started dilating again.

At exactly 6am on 21 June, I felt the need to push so I did. I heard my mum say, "It's a boy! You did it; you did it!" It was such an emotional moment. The look of relief and joy on Mum's face will stay with me forever. Kevin cried, he was so happy it was a boy and so happy we had a child; a child of our own.

We named him Lewis John Buhagiar, after Kevin's deceased dad. He was born at 6:05am on 21 June 2004, weighing eight pounds, four ounces and fifty centimeters tall. It's the shortest day of the year in Australia, but the happiest for us. We called our family and friends, and everyone was excited by the news.

Kevin and my mum stood by me during the whole five-year process of trying to have this baby. But as joy filled my heart, I still felt sadness for my daughter who never made the journey. I thought about what she would have looked like. Her name would have been Victoria Grace after my mum and my grandmother. I still think about her every day.

I tried IVF seven more times over the next eight years until the time came that we decided we'd had enough. We have Lewis, and we are more than grateful. Lewis is a kind and soft-hearted kid who will be turning twelve this year.

Writing this story has helped me understand the importance of life and the heartache that goes into being a parent. The journey was a long rough ride, but we got through it. We had support from our family and friends, and most of all we had each other.

kids they have or don't have, as every family has their own story.

So many people helped me on this journey. I wish to thank my husband Kevin, my mum, IVF Australia, Dr. Lovell, all the nurses at Nepean Private Hospital, my clinic nurse Anne, Dr. David Knight, Dr. Joel Bernstein, and our scientist Renee.

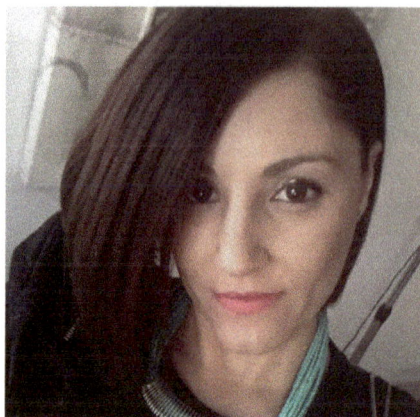

Jeanette Buhagiar

My name is Jeanette Buhagiar. I am 38 years old, mum to Lewis who is now 14 and live I in the Hawkesbury. I am a hairdresser and I also have a degree in skin science . Writing my story really helped me heal and complete my journey.

An Angel Nan's Story

I'm a mother of four grown children and currently grandmother of eight. Two of our daughters have had four losses between them in ten years, and my mum had four children from seven pregnancies. She told me often that you never forget those lost babies.

In March 2014, I saw a Facebook post by Fiona Kirk about starting an organisation to make baby burial garments from donated wedding dresses and felt immediately compelled to contact her. I was having chemotherapy following successful bowel cancer surgery and thought I could honour the lives of those babies by putting my professional dressmaking skills to good use, and joined Angel Gowns Australia

Since 2014, I've served as the Secretary, Co-Chair of the Seamstress Committee, and am still a board member as well as a seamstress and tutu maker with Angel Gowns Australia. I've been privileged to make many Special Requests for bereaved families. While this is rewarding, it can be especially challenging to know that those garments are for a particular baby or child, rather than stock for a hospital or funeral home.

My world shifted on its axis in November of 2017 when our own family suffered a terrible loss. My seventh grandchild, Elena Elisabeth, lived only for around forty-five minutes after being born very prematurely at twenty-two weeks and five days gestation.

My oldest daughter, Di, had arrived at my place several months earlier for an impromptu visit with her two children. They were wearing special T-shirts proclaiming they were a "future big sister" and a "future big brother." It took me a couple of minutes to understand what they meant, but what a happy surprise! My daughter gave a wry smile and admitted that she had only recently given away all her baby equipment, so she would have to start collecting again as baby was due in early April. My youngest daughter, Bron, was undergoing IVF treatment at the same time; not long after that, we were expecting two new babies in the family about a month apart. It was an exciting time for our family.

There was much planning, sharing of information, and baby tips passed between the sisters in the following months and they grew even closer than ever. However, in November, Di started to feel very unwell with a persistent fever and was seeing her specialist after some regular spotting. Scans showed that her little girl was safe. We were concerned but not alarmed.

One night, I took a terrible phone call from her husband, Steve, telling us that Di was in the hospital and that baby might have to be born prematurely. To be honest, we were in shock, but we drove to the hospital quickly, still hoping that with complete bed rest, the pregnancy would continue for a while longer.

By the time we arrived, Di had been moved to the birthing suite as she was already dilating and her amniotic fluid was leaking slowly. The midwife was so supportive, but frankly told my daughter that Baby would probably be stillborn or pass away just after birth due to her prematurity. Hospital protocol was not to offer resuscitation to babies under twenty-five weeks gestation, depending on their weight. As Di continued to get worse, her specialist recommended inducing labour immediately.

We left the hospital, and while hugging Di tightly, I whispered in her ear, "You've done your best, darling." What else can a mum say to her daughter in those circumstances?

So Elena Elisabeth was born in the early hours of 29th November 2017, weighing four hundred grams. My daughter and her husband were able to spend almost an hour cuddling and talking to her before she passed away in their arms.

When we received the message in the morning that Elena was born and had passed away, I think my heart broke into a million pieces for my baby granddaughter, my daughter, and all her family. They wanted to be left alone so I didn't meet Elena and have only seen one photo of her, taken by my son-in-law. She was perfect and looked just like her big sister; she was just way too early to live.

You hear stories about very preemie babies being hooked up to machines which keep them alive … they survive but have life-limiting disabilities. To be honest, I wouldn't have wished that for Elena, but the selfish part of me wishes that she could have had that chance.

Later analysis of swabs taken showed that Di had a serious Streptococcal B infection which caused the symptoms and possibly the pre-labour dilation and leak in the amniotic fluid. The consequences of prolonging the pregnancy could have been catastrophic for Di, so inducing labour was sadly the best option for them. What a terrible choice to have to make.

The days following Elena's death were a bit of a blur. We had to tell the rest of the family and close friends what had happened, and everyone was understandably very shocked and upset for us all. Elena's funeral was attended by her loving immediate family and best friends. Everyone was so supportive. Elena's big sister and big brother chose to come too.

The kids had been so excited to have a new baby coming and now were bewildered, especially our seven-year-old grandson who hadn't any experience with death and didn't really understand what had happened. He broke down when his dad spoke from the lectern directly to the kids, saying they would have been fantastic big sister and big brother to Elena. I was so proud of my son-in-law that day, showing his emotion but being so supportive of Di and the kids too.

I don't think I'll ever forget that day and the tiny white casket covered in baby roses on the table with a framed photo of Elena's little feet beside it. Elena's great auntie placed a pink teddy bear on the table as well, and that has since appeared in several family photos with her big sister and brother in honour of Elena.

I placed a little beaded angel I'd made amongst the baby roses on Elena's casket and saved a baby rose to dry and keep in my memory box. A personalised candle and Christmas bauble from Angel Gowns Australia sit on my shelf in tribute to Elena, but like the rest of our family, I'll never forget our little angel.

Every little life lost has a profound effect on not just the parents. Siblings, grandparents, extended family, and friends are all affected in their own way. As a grandparent and parent, I feel a double burden of grief for our lost little grandchild and her siblings, and for my daughter's heartache.

I'm so grateful that my daughter received amazing support from her midwife and the hospital staff at Blacktown Hospital where she was also given a package from Bears of Hope and an Angel Gowns Australia garment for Elena. White Lady Funerals was very compassionate in their arrangements, and it was such a comfort to have our family around us that day and in the months since Elena died. Di has said that they are grateful, as she knows that many relationships are strained and broken after such a tragic loss.

I believe that I'm now more empathetic than ever with anyone who has been affected by the death of a baby or young child. This may be when I'm writing a card to go with a Special Request I'm sending, sharing stories when attending events as a representative of Angel Gowns Australia, or in my everyday life. Breaking the silence about baby and infant loss and allowing people to recognise that child and speak freely about them is so important to everyone's health and well-being. I'm grateful that Melissa has included Elena's story in this book.

Christine McKenna

My husband John and I have been happily married for almost forty-five years and have an adult son and three daughters who are all married and have families of their own now.

I'm a professionally trained dressmaker and have sewn special occasion garments as well as a theatrical costume for many years. In 2014, I became a volunteer with Angel Gowns Australia and have served on the Management Committee as the Secretary and the Seamstress Committee.

My interest in historical clothing and Australian history has led me to some amazing opportunities over the years to be involved in special events and displays, and I volunteer at several historical properties in my region when I can. I have a large collection of antique and vintage women and children's clothing and have just started collecting vintage sewing machines.

For the past five years, I've have been a tutor at the local Community College in dressmaking, crochet, and macramé.

One Heart, Thrice Broken

It was one of the most beautiful images my husband and I had ever seen. I screamed, "Twins!" It was clear as day at my eight-week ultrasound appointment that there were two beautiful babies in my womb. After having an early miscarriage just six months prior, we felt so blessed to be given not one, but two babies. Tears of happiness flowed as we stared in amazement at our two new blessings.

I was immediately sent to a maternal-fetal medicine specialist (MFM) because of the type of twins my doctor presumed I was carrying, which was confirmed when the doctor announced they were monochorionic diamniotic twins: identical twins sharing the same placenta. Each baby was in its own amniotic sac. Both my OBGYN and MFM specialist would monitor me during my pregnancy.

Our families were overjoyed about the news of our twins. I beamed with pride, knowing I was carrying two precious little ones. A few weeks later, we found out we were having boys. How amazing to add two more boys to our burgeoning all-male family. This would make baby boys three and four. My pregnancy was going absolutely wonderful. I had no morning sickness and very little fatigue. I was on Cloud Nine.

During a routine check-up with my doctor at eighteen weeks, he noticed a large discrepancy in size between the twins, as well as an enlarged heart in one of the babies. He immediately scheduled an appointment with my MFM specialist to get specific details on the health of my boys. After a very in-depth ultrasound, we were told that our twins had stage four Twin to Twin Transfusion Syndrome.

Twin to Twin Transfusion Syndrome (TTTS) is when identical twins share unequal amounts of the placenta blood supply because of abnormal blood vessel connections between the twins and placenta. The blood flow through these blood vessel connections becomes unbalanced, resulting in the two fetuses growing at different rates, in turn causing various medical conditions to develop in the twins, such as hydrops, heart failure, dehydration, intrauterine growth restriction, anemia, and high blood pressure.

One twin is called the "recipient," who receives the majority of blood flow from the placenta, while the other twin is called the "donor," who receives very little blood flow from the placenta. Seventy percent of identical twins share a placenta, and fifteen to twenty percent of these pregnancies are affected by TTTS. There are five stages of TTTS. Stage five is when one or both twins have passed away.

We were overcome with shock, anger, confusion, and sadness. How could this be happening? Why was this not diagnosed sooner? My doctor proceeded to explain to us that there were only two options. First would be to do nothing at all and my twins would have a hundred percent mortality rate; or second, we would be to fly to Colorado and get an in-utero procedure done called fetoscopic laser ablation to attempt to seal the abnormal blood vessels causing the TTTS. We would do anything to save the lives of our babies. So, we chose to proceed with the fetoscopic laser ablation procedure and had to move extremely quick as the "recipient" baby had severe heart failure and could pass at any moment. Three hours later, my husband and I were on a plane to Colorado.

We arrived in Colorado on a very frigid and sombre evening. We sat in the cab still in shock; even silent words were too loud to speak. We eventually arrived at our destination, the Children's Hospital of Colorado, where I was whisked away for a series of tests to see just how extensive the TTTS had progressed. Matias, my recipient baby, was in heart failure, had hydrops, polyhydramnios, and an eighty percent placental share. Mael, my donor baby, was anemic, thirty percent smaller than his brother, had intrauterine growth restriction, oligohydramnios, and a mere twenty percent placental share. The following morning, I was scheduled to complete the in-utero fetoscopic laser ablation procedure to save my precious boys, Matias and Mael.

I was wheeled into the operating room; it felt like something out of a horror movie. The twenty staff members in their blue scrubs and masks surrounded me, and I could hear classical music playing throughout the operating room while bright lights were shining in my face. I remember the loud beeping and humming coming from the medical equipment that monitored the twins and me. I had never been so nervous, scared, and unprepared of what was to come. The medical staff had three lives in their hands, all we could do was have faith in God and pray for the best outcome.

The procedure was to only take an hour to complete but ended up being a three-hour procedure. I was in and out of consciousness; at one point toward the end of the procedure, I woke up on the operating table. I vaguely remember hearing the doctors discussing my babies' heartbeats. I asked the anesthesiologist who was sitting nearby, "Are my babies okay?" She told me my babies were both alive, but that the doctors were unable to complete the procedure.

The doctors waited until I was completely awake to explain exactly what had happened. My husband and I were told that three incisions were made into my stomach, and as soon as the doctors entered into my womb, I had myometrial bleeding at the entry site. I started to bleed into the twins amniotic sacs, causing the once clear fluid to become so cloudy they were unable to see the placenta. Doctors attempted to remove the cloudy amniotic fluid by replacing it with clear fluid, but to no avail. Unfortunately, after several attempts, the doctors were unsuccessful in getting the amniotic fluid clear enough to proceed with the laser ablation procedure.

Again, we had to quickly move forward and discuss our options in hopes to save Matias and Mael. The doctors told us we had three options. The first was to do nothing and let nature take its course. My twins would soon pass away on their own. Second, would be selective reduction. We would have to sacrifice one of the twins to potentially save the other twin's life—they suggested we terminate our recipient baby, Matias. Lastly, we could attempt the laser ablation procedure once again the next day. This option had far more complications since it had just been attempted, and the outcome was unsuccessful. However, the first and second choices weren't options for me.

I couldn't fathom the thought of taking the life of my own child. Without hesitation, my decision was made. I wanted the doctors to perform the procedure again.

Déjà vu? Groundhog Day, perhaps? There I was, the very next morning, being whisked right back into that same cold, bright, blue scrub staff-filled, classical music-playing room.

Again, what was supposed to take an hour, took three hours. Once the anesthesia wore off, they told my husband and me that the second procedure was successful and that both babies were alive. They advised us that the next twenty-four hours would be the most crucial, as many babies have passed away during this time period after having the procedure done.

I was scheduled for an ultrasound the next day. There was no doubt in my mind everything was well and Matias and Mael were thriving. The first baby the doctor checked during the ultrasound was Matias, the recipient, and he had a strong and beautiful heartbeat. Within hours of the procedure, Matias had already started to heal from his heart failure and hydrops.

I asked the doctor, "Is there a heartbeat on Mael?"

The doctor paused for a moment and with hesitation said, "I'm sorry, but there is no heartbeat."
I looked at my husband, shaking my head vigorously with my legs flailing under the sheets. My husband kept saying, "No, I won't believe that." Eventually, the staff exited the room, giving us time alone. There were no words spoken; there was nothing to say, we sat petrified. Internally, I knew I had to continue to fight for the "survivor," Matias. I would have to remain strong and continue to carry both babies in my womb until Matias was due.

We stayed in Colorado for six more days. After several echocardiograms, ultrasounds, and MRI's, the doctors cleared me to fly back home. Matias continued to heal and became healthier every day. I was put on strict bed rest until it was time to give birth. Doctors feared that I would have preterm premature rupture of membranes (PPROM), because of the six incisions from the two laser ablation procedures. I often thought of the bittersweet day that I would give birth to my boys, knowing that only one would be alive and the other would be born sleeping.

After two weeks of being on strict bed rest, I noticed a decrease in fetal movement with Matias. My husband and I immediately went to the hospital. They monitored his heart, and we were cleared to go home, as all seemed well. Two days passed, and as I was getting my oldest son ready for school, again, I felt no movement. Although I had a doctor's appointment that afternoon with my MFM specialist, I was told to come in immediately. As I was getting the ultrasound, I asked the sonographer if she could see the baby's heartbeat.

She said, "I'm having trouble finding it."

She then left the room to find the doctor. As I waited for the doctor, tears immediately began to fall from my eyes. I knew what they were going to tell me once again. Moments later, the doctor walked in and told us that Matias had most likely passed away that night as I slept. I can't quite put my feelings into words at this point. They were simply indescribable; the pain was unbearable. My heart was once again broken.

The next morning I was scheduled to be induced and give birth to my twins. After a tearful, prayerful, and sleepless night we headed to the hospital. We had yet to tell our older sons what was happening. We told them while at the hospital, right before I was to be induced. My oldest son was heartbroken, which ripped me to pieces even more.

On the 29th of October, 2014, after thirteen long hours of labor, I gave birth to two beautifully perfect boys. Matias Yanai and Mael Nasir Johnson. They resembled their older brothers so much. They had perfect feet, the cutest hands, and adorable button noses. Matias was big enough to cradle Mael in his arms. We spent one and a half days with our handsome boys; we bathed and put lotion on them, we held and loved on them. I even sang to them. My husband and I had portraits taken of the four of us. Family members came to visit them and our pastor came and blessed them. I didn't want our time together to end. I could have held them forever.

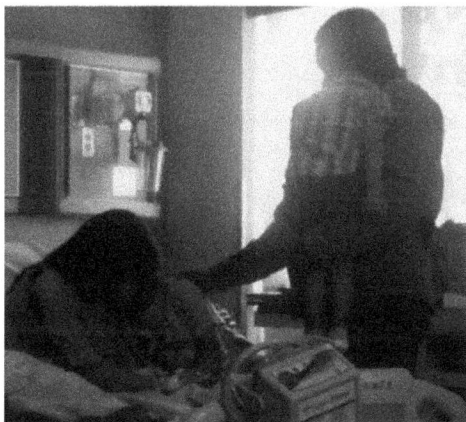

Planning and arranging for their cremation was difficult and painful. Instead of choosing what cute matching outfits to bring them home in, we had to choose a funeral home that would provide the services we needed for our boys. We watched as the funeral staff drove off with Matias and Mael. I had just given birth to two beautiful boys, yet I left with empty arms.

Matias and Mael opened the eyes of my heart. They allowed me to see the beauty in things I never knew were there. I will be forever changed. Missing them never ends, my love for them is everlasting. It will never grow old or ever fade away. They will always carry a piece of my heart with them in heaven.

As a mother of angel babies, one of my biggest fears is that our babies will be forgotten. I try my hardest to do things to honor Matias, Mael, and our early loss baby, whom we named Angel.

My breast milk came in three days after having my twins. After giving it great thought, instead of stopping my milk from continuing to produce, I decided to pump and donate it. I found a local group that connects you with mothers who are in need of breast milk for their babies. I pumped religiously every three to four hours for three months. I donated my milk to a ten-month-old baby girl named Holly.

Yes, at times I broke down, thinking to myself, This milk should be for my boys. In retrospect, I believe it was the best decision for me. It helped my healing process and most importantly, honored Matias and Mael.

All of the clothing that my boys have ever worn in and while leaving the hospital were either sewn or knitted and donated by churches, individuals, or foundations. My plan is to make clothing for smaller babies, such as Matias & Mael, and donate the clothing to hospitals.

For their birthday every year, we donate memory boxes to the hospital where they were born. I received the same memory boxes to take home when I gave birth to Matias and Mael. We tailor our boxes with items we think may shine some light upon these mothers who are going through one of the darkest times of their life. We attach a small note saying they were donated in memory of our children.

Since having Matias and Mael, I have given birth to two more children. I am so thankful and overcome with joy, for all of my children. I want to tell all the mothers to be, mothers to come, and mothers whose children left this world way too soon to never lose hope. Do not let fear steal your joy for the future. May God bless you on your journey and give you strength, comfort, peace, and hope.

Shalina Johnson

Shalina Johnson is a mother of seven children. She has been married for eight years to Mustafa Johnson. She and her family reside in Phoenix, Arizona USA.

Shalina has experienced the loss of three children; one to miscarriage and twins who were stillborn. Through her journey, she is motivated to be of assistance to other parents who will, unfortunately, go through child loss as well.

Shalina is currently in the process of becoming a doula that specializes in bereavement and will further her education in sonography.

Nay-Nay, Our Early Arriver

I have a wonderful husband whom I've been with since we were sixteen and two beautiful children. We have a son, Bayley, who is eleven years old, and a daughter who is now nine years old (going on twenty-five!).

Our son was born on the 2nd of September 2007. I had a normal thirty-eight-week pregnancy, despite bad heartburn, horrible morning sickness, and terribly, agonizing pelvic pain. Oh, and that my labour was twenty-two hours long—on Fathers' Day! But I can't complain, as all went well.

I became pregnant with our daughter a year and a half later.

My pregnancy was going great. I had my gynaecologist appointment on the 28th of August 2009 and everything was perfect. I was told I could deliver the baby in about five week's time from that appointment. We were pretty excited.

We had a friend's birthday party on the 31st of August 2009.

There was a jumping castle—of course, my son was one of the first on it. He loves them! Lunch was ready to be served, and I went to get my son off the jumping castle, but being a kid he jumped off the jumping castle and into my arms. I thought nothing of it, as he always did that. I felt a slight pull in my lower abdomen, not painful at all. I forgot about it, as it didn't give me any trouble afterwards.

A few days later, on the 1st of September 2009, when I was thirty-one and half weeks pregnant, I was casually reading a book to our soon-to-be two-year-old son. I felt a dull, heavy period-like ache in my lower abdomen and lower back. It took me by surprise, as I hadn't felt this ache much during this pregnancy. I got up quite quickly, and as soon as I did, I felt a huge watery gush appear from me. I was wearing black pants, so I assumed my waters broke.

Standing in the hallway, I rang hubby straight away to come home. He was working about forty minutes away from home. Had it been the day before, he would have been only five minutes away—isn't that always the way?!

As soon as I went to the bathroom, I noticed it wasn't my waters. It was blood! So much of it, it looked pretty scary! Meanwhile, my son was in his room still looking at the book I had been reading him.

I stayed very calm, as I remembered if Mum stays calm, so does baby. I rang emergency immediately. The emergency call operator was so lovely and kept me calm throughout the whole ordeal. Funny enough, I was in absolutely no pain whatsoever.

She asked me where I was. I replied by saying I was sitting on the toilet as blood was gushing out like a tap. I didn't want to freak my son out if he saw what was happening! She told me that I had to get off the toilet as baby could be born any minute. At that point, I kind of started to panic ... but still, kept myself quite calm for my son's and my unborn baby's sakes.

The operator asked me to get some towels, but I had no towels in the bathroom at that moment. I was running through the house, pouring blood (sorry for the graphic detail); there were pools of blood throughout my house. It looked terrifying!

After what seemed like a long time but was actually about seven minutes, I heard the ambulance sirens. Thank goodness, thank goodness, I kept saying to myself. But of course, the front door was locked. So holding the bloodied towel below and hopping over to the front door as quickly as I could, I unlocked it to find two male ambulance guys standing there. I had no time to be embarrassed; I was just so grateful they were there to help my baby and me!
The ambulance, of course, caused a stir on my quiet street. One of my beautiful neighbour's came over to look after my son while I was rushed to the hospital, and then called my mother to stay with our son, which I am very grateful for. My neighbour also cleaned up after me, which she didn't have to do at all. I am forever grateful for all who helped me that day.

As the ambulance officers were putting me on the stretcher, I was asked which hospital I preferred, Blacktown or Mt. Druitt. I had a bad experience with Blacktown years before, so I was very hesitant to go there. They persuaded me to go to Blacktown, as I was going to have this baby in ten minutes!

As soon as I was lying in the back of the ambulance, I started getting contractions and pretty strong ones too. This baby of ours was obviously ready to make her entrance. On my way to the hospital, while being checked over by the lovely ambulance officers, all I could think was, Please let my baby be healthy.

When I arrived at the hospital, I was rushed in to have an

emergency caesarean. My hubby was nowhere in sight, although—unknown to me—he was rushing to get to us like a crazy man.

Some of the staff did not seem very friendly. My nail polish had to be removed for the emergency caesarean, and I made a small joke to the nurse removing it: "Oh, you get the fun job." She rolled her eyes and totally ignored me. I said out loud, "Geez, anyone would think that you're the one on the surgery table!" Maybe it wasn't the time or place to joke around, but that's just how I am.

I was desperate to see my husband, but he arrived ten minutes after I was taken into theatre. I was devastated that my husband missed the birth of our baby.

I was given a full anesthetic, so I couldn't say how long I was out for or even who performed the surgery. When I finally awoke, I had no idea if my baby was okay or not. They had put me in a room with no windows or anything, and the lights were very dimmed. I called for a nurse to take me to see my baby. I know how busy nurses are, so I completely understand why they didn't rush to me. But for me, this was a huge deal! I desperately wanted to meet my baby and just know that she was okay.

Finally, after fifteen to twenty minutes, a nurse came in and abruptly responded, "What do you want?"

I couldn't believe how rude they were to me after the ordeal I had just gone through. Meanwhile, as I was waiting for someone to take me to see my daughter, I heard the staff laughing and joking around right outside my door. It was unbelievable.

At this stage, the doctor came in and told me that I had placenta abruption. I had read so much about placenta abruption, but I never thought it would happen to me! The doctor said to me that it usually only happens to people who are heavy smokers, drug users, and alcoholics! I don't ever touch any of those things, so they can throw that theory out the window.

The nurse finally took me to see our daughter. The first person I saw was my amazing husband. I just cried when I saw him. He had actually met our daughter before I did. We went in together for me to meet our beautiful baby girl for the first time. After seeing my little princess covered in tubes and wires, lying there helpless in the humidity crib, we just didn't know what to expect.

Being wheeled in, pale and weak as I was, I met our beautiful daughter. I fell in love the moment I saw her. We named her Shonaya. Despite all the tubes and wires attached to her, she was perfect. She did need a little help with breathing, so she needed the CPAP. Shonaya weighed one point seven kilograms. She was so tiny. But overall, she was a good weight to be at eight weeks' premature, which was in her favour. And boy, she had a set of lungs on her!

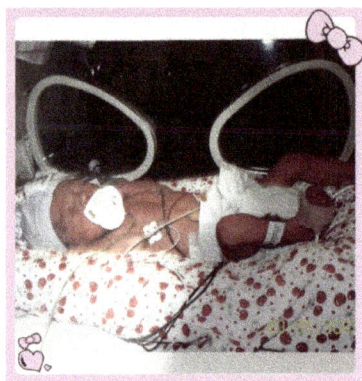

We weren't allowed to hold our precious baby yet. So we did miss out on a lot of things, such as photos of her birth, being able to hear her cry for the first time, giving her her first sip of breast milk and even just holding her. But she was in great care.

So just after five minutes of meeting Shonaya, of course, there was always one nurse who had to be quite blunt. While the nurse was leaning on the humidity crib where my daughter lay, she gazed at me and said very abruptly, "Now you know she could possibly die, don't you?" I looked at her and didn't know what to say; my eyes filled with tears. I was gobsmacked! I think we all knew that it was a possibility, but all I kept thinking was positive vibes. I didn't want a person like that around my baby!

A head nurse approached me and asked what happened as another nurse overheard the conversation. I told her what was said. I clearly stated that I believe people with attitudes like that should not be in positions of caring for other people who are unwell or who have been through traumatic situations.

I know nurse's jobs are huge and have a great deal of significance in our communities. I have so much respect for doctors and nurses, but only the ones who have compassion, sympathy, and thoughtfulness towards their patients. It's called humanity. Unfortunately, many people lack it.

I'm not sure what happened after that, as all I was concerned about was our daughter. I was taken back to the dimmed room, which made me feel uneasy. A nurse came in and without giving me any local anesthetic, pulled out my catheter out there and then. I was in so much pain that I grabbed her hand and said some unsavoury words. Not meaning to be rude to the nurse, but the pain I was in was worse than natural labour!

Most of it is a blur after that traumatic ordeal. The next thing I remember is being taken to RPA hospital by ambulance to spend the next two weeks with our baby girl. My husband said that they were going to send us to Melbourne if they couldn't find us a bed in Sydney. Thankfully they did!

Once we arrived at RPA, I wasn't feeling my usual self. I was quite depressed and missing my husband and our son so much. Being alone in a place where you know no one can be pretty daunting. I had to share a room where the lady didn't speak a word of English, so it made it so hard to make a friend while there.

I clearly remember the lady I was sharing a room with had brought in her other children who were sick with the flu into my room also. So that made me quite nervous, as I was frightened Shonaya would become unwell.

I was sad all the time. I just didn't want to be there. But I was so grateful for all the nurses and doctors who were looking after our baby girl. I just wanted to be home with my new baby, son, and husband.

One of the counselors came to speak to me. She allowed me to go home on the weekends. This was such a huge relief for me, but I was constantly crying because I just felt so down and hated leaving my baby there without me.

After two weeks, I started feeling better, although I was still in pain from the C-section.

We were then transferred to Norwest private hospital in Bella Vista, our daughter's home for another two weeks. With help from my husband, mother, and mother-in-law driving me back and forth for feeding times, I was in much better spirits, and Shonaya was doing so well.

Every day our daughter was improving and getting bigger and stronger. It was such a great feeling! After two weeks, Shonaya was able to come home, even though she was still so small at just thirty-six weeks' gestation. I was quite strict about having any visitors at this point, as I was afraid of Shonaya becoming unwell. We were just over the moon that after all our little family went through, we came out stronger in the end, especially our little Shonaya.

Shonaya is now nine years old and full of laughs, attitude and lots of energy! The way it should be.

I know so many mothers and fathers don't have the same outcome that we did. So I would like to send all my love, strength, positive energy, and support to all who are going through such hard times and heartache with pregnancy/birth related issues. I wish each and every person reading this the very best outcome in becoming parents. Never give up.

Martina Vassallo

I'm Martina, a busy mum of three children. I met my love when we were sixteen years old, been together for nineteen years and married for thirteen. We have two boys and a girl; eldest is Bayley who's eleven yrs old, Shonaya who's nine years old, and little Ashtyn who is eleven months old.

I've had my own home-based business called MaR-Valicious BiteS since 2010, baking and decorating biscuits for all occasions. I also have an online store specializing in cookie cutters. I, unfortunately, struggle with daily chronic pain. I was only recently diagnosed with a rare genetic autoimmune disease along with other painful conditions.

I have three siblings; my eldest sister is Melissa Desveaux, creator of this beautiful book. I am an identical twin to Rebecca, well, mirror-image twins actually, which is really fun. We are so different but so alike. We also have a younger brother Mat, who's crazily hilarious and witty, who lives all the way over in London.

I couldn't be prouder of all my siblings. I am so grateful that we all share a close, caring bond with each other. Life certainly is very busy, but I wouldn't change it for the world!

Our Precious Twins Complete Our Family

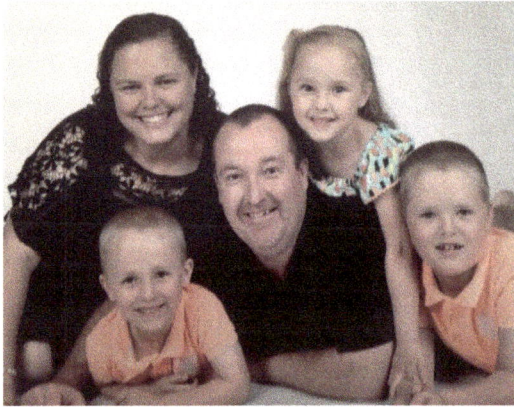

It was our son James' first birthday. We had decided that once he turned one, we would try for baby number two, as we wanted a fairly close age gap.

It had taken us about six months to fall pregnant with James. It had been a normal pregnancy besides the horrendous morning sickness that stayed with me for the whole pregnancy. James was born via spontaneous labour at thirty-five weeks. I was still working as a teacher at the time and had another two weeks of work before my maternity leave started. He was born after a fourteen-hour labour and a vacuum extraction, weighing a healthy two thousand, seven hundred and eighty grams. James spent five days in the SCN (Special Care Nursery) and was initially being tube fed. On the fourth day, he learned to suck feed and was able to come home.

Months went by and there was no positive pregnancy test. I saw my doctor who referred me to an obstetrician. I was diagnosed with PCOS after having some tests and the doctor said that we were most likely to need some help to fall pregnant. We decided to give it a few more months and did everything possible to help our chances. We changed our diet drastically and ate a very healthy balanced diet, including fish and nuts. We exercised daily and both lost over twenty kilograms of weight. We took vitamin supplements and followed every old wives' tale, took on every bit of advice; but still, no luck. The doctor prescribed me metformin and clomid to ensure I ovulated every month, as the blood tests had shown that wasn't always the case. I continued taking them for four months, with no success. I then tried acupuncture for fertility, which was successful in making me ovulate, but not fall pregnant.

After eighteen months, we were referred to the Sydney IVF clinic. We were hesitant to go, but we would have done anything to get a brother or sister for James. We went along to the appointment worried and nervous. The obstetrician referred us to "the best IVF doctor" as he said, and even though he was an hour away from us, we were willing to try. After doing some tests and an ultrasound of both me and my husband, we were told that it was highly unlikely that we would be able to conceive naturally. He gave us only a two percent chance.

We left the appointment disheartened but determined to keep trying. As two percent was better than zero percent, we decided we would continue trying for another six months on our own before beginning the IVF process.

This was a bit of a relief for us. We relaxed a bit. We knew that if in six months I was not pregnant, we would go back to the IVF clinic and begin the process. I think your emotional state plays a big part in the conception process. Because three months later, a home pregnancy test confirmed I was pregnant. All on our own! No help needed.

I went to my GP, who did a blood test to confirm the pregnancy. When the results were back, she said to me, "You are either a lot further along than four weeks, or you are having twins. Your HCG levels are quite high." I jokingly laughed and told her that I was sure of my dates, but there couldn't possibly be more than one baby.

From four weeks onwards, I was constantly nauseous and sick. I was vomiting up to ten times a day and couldn't even keep down water. I ended up going to the emergency department at the hospital twice because I was so dehydrated. Each time, they admitted me and put me on a drip of fluids and Maxolon, rehydrated me, and then sent me home. I had to come back daily after being sent home for a few hours a day on a drip.

I had an appointment with my obstetrician when I was seven weeks pregnant. He was happy for us, as we hadn't needed to take the IVF route. He had an ultrasound machine in his room and did an ultrasound, hoping to see a sac and a heartbeat. Before the ultrasound, he said to us, "The last two patients of mine today have found out that they are having twins. I wonder if you will be the third." We laughed and said, "Yeah yeah, as if that would happen to us!"

Once the ultrasound started, I immediately saw two distinct sacs on the screen. He shook my husband's hand and said, "Congratulations, you are having twins." We were in disbelief. How could this be? We could only laugh and tell him there must be a problem with his machine. But it was true; we were having twins! All on our own!

The pregnancy was a difficult one. I was diagnosed with hyper emesis gravid arum, as my morning sickness was so severe. I had to take eight weeks' sick leave from work; there was no way I could teach a class without running out multiple times a day to vomit. I was also diagnosed with gestational diabetes and had to be monitored through the high-risk clinic at the hospital because of a multiple birth, previous premature birth, and diabetes.

The ultrasound confirmed we were having Dichorionic/ Diamniotic (di/di) twins. Di/di twins are the most common type of twins and the lowest risk. Di/di twins can be identical if the egg split very early, but fraternal twins are always di/ di. Our twins were fraternal di/di twins; each twin had their own placenta and their own amniotic sac. Di/di twin pregnancies have increased risks over single pregnancies, but this is the best case scenario in twin world. The biggest worry was going into preterm labour and making sure both babies were growing adequately.

My aim was always to get to thirty-four weeks so I could deliver at my local hospital and so my babies would have the best chance of survival. At thirty-two weeks and six days, I went into labour. I was having contractions, and I was two centimeters dilated. I went to the hospital, which confirmed that I was in labour. But they told me I could not have the babies there, as there were too many premature babies to be cared for. They told me that they would ring around to find the closest hospital that had available beds.

A short while later, they said that they had two beds in Canberra. I asked them to keep trying, as I wanted to stay in Sydney if possible. They came back to me and said they had one NICU bed in Liverpool and one in Royal North Shore, so I could deliver at Liverpool, but one baby would be sent to the other hospital. That wasn't good enough, and after persisting with them, they got two NICU beds in Liverpool. They put me in an ambulance and transferred me to Liverpool, and gave me tocolytic drugs to stop the labour. The drugs worked. Labour stopped, and everything seemed good.

They kept me in hospital for twenty-four hours and then sent me home. We thought we had escaped a premature birth.

WRONG! A few hours after getting home, my waters broke in bed. They were on their way. This time I went straight to Liverpool. They gave me a shot of steroids and an anti-D injection for my negative Rhesus blood type.

I laboured for twelve hours and then was so exhausted that I could not go on. I decided to have an epidural, and it was heaven. I finally felt like I was in control and knew what was going on. At 4:45pm, the first twin, Harrison, was born. By this stage, I had an audience of eleven people in the room! An obstetrician, two midwives, two pediatricians, two pediatric nurses and four students, plus us! Harrison was born and needed to be rubbed up before he cried. He was shown to me and then taken away to the neonatal intensive care nursery. I was told he was fine and weighed two thousand and forty grams.

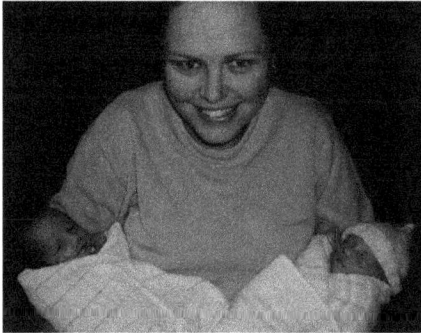

The second twin, Emily, was in no hurry to come at all. She was high up under my ribs and her water had not broken. The midwife broke her waters, and then tried to physically push her down into the birth canal. After thirty-eight minutes of contractions and pushing, Emily was finally born at 5:23pm. She was wrapped up and taken away to NICU as well. She weighed a tiny eighteen hundred and ninety grams.

Harrison and Emily both spent twenty-four hours on CPAP (continuous positive airway pressure) to help with breathing, then three days in a humid crib. They were tube fed and had some trouble regulating their body temperature. After four days, they were transferred via ambulance from the NICU at

Liverpool to the SCN at Campbelltown Hospital. They spent three weeks there, growing and learning to suck feed. It was a difficult time, having three-year-old James to look after, as well as spending days and nights at the hospital.

After three weeks, the twins were finally home. Our family was complete, and the fun was just starting! The first twelve months were difficult. They both had reflux, screamed lots, and didn't sleep much. Emily was diagnosed with renal kidney reflux so had a few hospital stays and medical appointments that kept us busy.

But we are a family, and we are over the moon with happiness!

Alicia Sinfield

My name is Alicia Sinfield, and I am a wife, mother of three, and primary school teacher. I am very blessed and fortunate to have three healthy and happy children, and although it wasn't the easiest ride to get here, it was in no way as tough as many others in the book had to endure.

I hope my story can give hope to those trying to conceive, those who are pregnant with multiples, and those who have had a premature baby. Much love to you all.

Ava Grace - Birth Story

The staff assigned for Ava's birth are some of the most compassionate people I have ever met.

They pass the tissues as I cry hysterically about how unfair this all is. They listen as I let out a gut-wrenching roar from deep within about not even eating a piece of deli meat or seafood during this pregnancy. They hold my hand and agree with me that this is the worst situation you can be in. They run and grab me vomit bags time and time again and agree that it shouldn't have been that I have also had to go through hyper emesis gravid arum for the entire pregnancy, yet don't get to hold a warm, wriggling baby in the end. They hold my hand as they give me needles and other medications to help with the relentless nausea, which is a combination of extreme fear, panic, sadness, shock, morning sickness, and morphine.

They bring my husband meals, which he cannot eat, but we are grateful for the gesture. They tell me I can do this, that I am strong, that I will get to meet my daughter soon. They say her name, her beautiful name, over and over again. They come running when I push my button in sheer panic when my waters break, screaming for them to call my obstetrician.

They calm me with soothing words and again affirm that I can do this, that I will meet my precious daughter soon.

They listen through my sobs about the plans we had for our daughter and our family that was supposed to have five people in it soon. They check me calmly as I begin to enter the final stage of labour, knowing that the end of the birthing process is near. They whisper to my husband to quickly go and tell the staff on the desk to call my obstetrician to come now, the baby's birth is imminent! They hold my tiny daughter for what feels like hours in a way so that she isn't born before I am ready and not before the obstetrician arrives. As we are waiting, they describe my daughter's dainty features.

The obstetrician arrives. He is the same one who delivered my son and older daughter over the past few years; in my eyes, he is the best obstetrician in the world. Calmly, he delivers my third child.

Her birth is silent. The room is silent. There are no tears. There are no cheers. The obstetrician describes in detail what she looks like, asking gently if we want to see her. My husband and I look at each other with a glance, both knowing the answer in that second. Yes please, we want to see her, we want to hold her and never let her go. We want to cuddle her, and love on her, and kiss her. She's handed to me, all fifteen point five centimeters and one hundred and five grams, to hold after a two and a half hour labour.

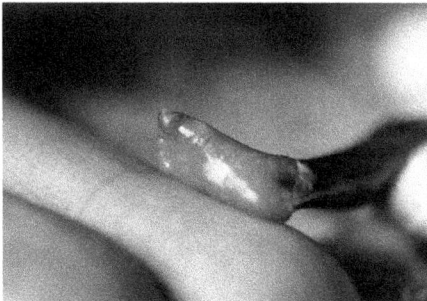

I'm exhausted, emotionally and physically, but I'm smiling, I'm actually grinning ear to ear, just as if I'd given birth to a full term, healthy baby. I am in such awe about what a perfectly formed little girl we have created. I am so happy to meet her and hold her.

At the same moment that my heart is being shattered into a million pieces, my heart is also full. My husband reaches out to touch her. I see the deep pain but also so much love for our third child. The midwife and obstetrician have tears in their eyes and comment how beautiful she is. She really is beautiful.

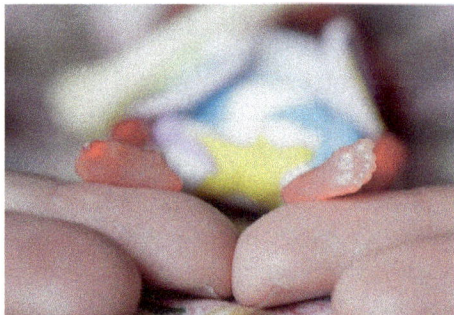

Ava died because of fatal birth defects. We have heard the term "incompatible with life" said many times before and after her birth, but those words (which I hate) don't take away anything from her beauty. They don't take away from the fact that she always had a place in our family. That she was supposed to be born.

How amazing that at fifteen weeks and three days gestation she has ten tiny fingers and toes. She has her sister's chin, she has her daddy's toes, she has her brother's fingers, and she has my knees. Her knuckles are all there, and her fingernails are formed. Two tiny ears, two tiny eyes, and a perfect little mouth. Just a tiny baby. Our baby.

AVA GRACE JOHNSON. Monday 16th March 2015.
Born still, but still born.

Psalm 139:13-16 (NIV)
For you created my inmost being; you knit me together in my mother's womb. I praise you because I am fearfully and wonderfully made; your works are wonderful, I know that full well. My frame was not hidden from you when I was made in the secret place, when I was woven together in the depths of the earth. Your eyes saw my unformed body; all the

days ordained for me were written in your book before one of them came to be.

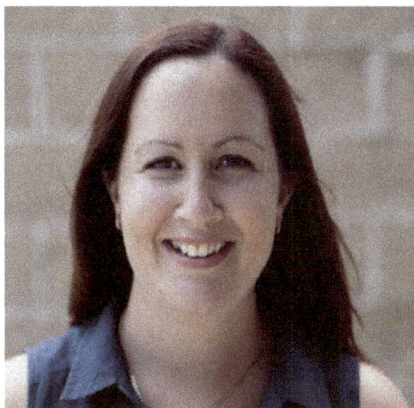

Erin Johnson

Erin Johnson is an advocate for compassionate bereavement care for families and their babies who have passed away before soon after birth. A wife, mother, primary school teacher, blogger, and volunteer, Erin founded Ava Grace No Footprint Too Small after experiencing the loss of her daughter, Ava Grace, in the second trimester of pregnancy in 2015.

Through her community group, Ava Grace No Footprint Too Small, Erin has rallied volunteers from all over Australia to sew, knit, and crochet baby clothes and blankets for thousands of families experiencing the loss of a baby. Thousands of baby clothes, hats, teddies, nappies, blankets, and keepsakes have been donated to hospitals around Australia to be gifted to bereaved parents so that they can dress their baby.

Through her blog and Facebook group, Erin has created a global online community which provides support, connection, and acknowledgement of infant loss. Erin strives to break the silence surrounding miscarriage, stillbirth, and infant loss by sharing Ava Grace's story and by empowering other women and families to share their personal journeys of grief.

Our Precious Gem - Ruby
22-11-14

I hadn't been feeling well all week. All I could think was, "God, it can't be that long until labour and this baby comes out."

I was admitted to our little local hospital on 16 November 2014, with a high heart rate and feeling "blah." I was booked in for my routine scan the next day. That night, I got no sleep, I was hungry, I ate, I threw up, and then the fire alarm went off—someone was having a hot shower, and the steam set the alarm off. The next morning, I couldn't wait to get out of there, although the staff was nice and all. But who wants to stay in hospital?

That Monday morning after my drip was taken out and I was getting ready to be released, I asked the nurse if what they had given me to try and stop the nausea and vomiting could possibly have had an adverse reaction and be the cause of me feeling bruised all over. Unknown to anyone, this was my body starting to shut down.

Kyle, my husband, had to work that day, as he had not long started his dream job. So Mum—ah, thank god for my mum!—came with me to my scan which was forty-five minutes away. The baby was fine, all well, although he or she (we chose not to find out the sex) hadn't put on much weight, but we just put that down to me not being able to keep anything down. My mother-in-law was also present at the scan. She was so excited to see her grandchild moving around on the screen and most importantly, hearing the heartbeat.

I had an appointment with my GP on 20 November 2014. This was just a check-up after my overnight stay on Sunday. He got the Doppler out, and we heard the baby's heartbeat for what was to be the very last time.

We didn't know the gender of our sweet baby. It was going to be a surprise, a way for me to get through my labour—that was my train of thought, anyway.

On 21 November 2014, I was sick, sick, sick. I thought that this might be the day. I couldn't keep anything down, not even water. I felt like absolute crap; I would lie down and not be able to get comfortable and would throw up again and again, time after time. I didn't have any specific pain, but I ached all over. I just thought that this was me and how I was when I'm pregnant.

Kyle came home at lunchtime; he was passing through town and decided he would check on me. I can remember he told me I looked like crap. Mum also called in and said the same.

At about 10:30pm, I rang Mum and told her that I just didn't feel right. I had been telling this to Kyle, but he was so exhausted from his new job he just wanted to go to bed and sleep. I can still hear Mum's voice: "Well, I suggest if you don't feel right, you go to hospital or at least ring the maternity ward. You have their number, don't you?" I agreed with her and rang the maternity ward at the hospital where I was going to give birth.

I wish I could remember the lady's name; she was lovely (insert sarcasm). I told her of my concerns to which she replied, "Sounds like you're just not handling the pain that goes with labour." Okie dokie then! I asked her if I should come in; she said I could if I wanted to. I said, "Okay, well, we will be there in about an hour."

I then went and broke the news to my husband, and he wasn't all that impressed. I grabbed the baby's hospital bag, and Kyle grabbed mine and his. I rang Mum to let her know that we were heading to the hospital.

On the way, we discussed and finalised boy's and girl's names. We laughed about the fact that we were driving the ute, which hadn't yet had the baby capsule installed. We were so excited that this could be it; this could be the beginning of us being parents.

We arrived at the hospital around 11:15pm. It was dark and pretty quiet for a Friday night. We were taken up to the maternity ward—well, actually, we were given directions on how to get there. I explained again to a group of midwives what had been happening.

The first thing they did was lay me down and check my blood pressure, which was fine. They did a urine test; also fine. Then it was time to be put on the heartbeat machine. We were still pretty excited. The midwife spent a couple of minutes moving the belly bands around, trying to find the baby's heartbeat. She said she had found it but was going to get one of the gynecologists to come in and have a good listen. We still weren't worried. It didn't even occur to us that anything horrible could go wrong.

The gynecologist came in with a portable ultrasound machine. He tried to find the heartbeat but couldn't. He told us that someone must have been fiddling with the dials on the laptop, so he went to find the other machine. He still couldn't find our baby's heartbeat. After this, I can't remember much, although I do recall being told that they were going to call the "head honcho" in as he would be the best bet at finding the heartbeat. Kyle held my hand.

Suddenly, we heard the most stupid, ridiculous, unthinkable sentence any parents could ever hear: "I'm sorry, I can't find the heartbeat, there is no heartbeat, I am so very sorry." These words shouldn't even exist.

I said in a very stern voice, "Excuse me? What? You have to be joking!"

Kyle just fell to the floor and started crying. My heart broke. Actually, it shattered into a million bloody freaking pieces.

After a moment—or maybe a million—I asked what was going to happen now. After another scan to confirm our precious baby had no heartbeat, we were told to think about a few things, including whether to be induced or go home and wait? Pain relief? Calling family?

We decided to be induced. I wanted to meet our baby. And I wanted pain relief; if my baby was going to be stillborn, I wasn't going to go through the physical pain if I could help it.

We were taken to a lovely room away from all the crying babies. This is where we made the phone calls. Kyle called his parents and I called mine. We cried. We cried a lot. My parents came straight to the hospital. I will never be able to erase the looks on Mum's and Dad's faces as they walked through the door.

Kyle slept; he must have been buggered. Mum rubbed my back and Dad sat in a chair, devastated. Mum, Dad, and Kyle were there the whole time for which I will never be able to thank them enough.

I had my first lot of induction gel at around 3:30am. It was gross. And this is about all I actually remember.

Our midwife, Lauren, was doing my observations and getting ready for my second lot of gel when my heart rate plummeted and my blood pressure went through the roof. She had to call for help.

I do remember walking—because I wasn't going anywhere in a wheelchair—down the hall with my hospital gown wide open to the room where they were going to prepare me for an emergency C-section. Three nurses had trouble putting the catheter in; I had only produced about three milliliters of urine over a long period of time and my kidneys had shut down. Bloods also showed that my liver function was on its way out too. I was now in multi-organ failure. It must have been scary, scary stuff for Kyle, Mum, and Dad. They had just lost a child and grandchild and were now facing the possibility of losing a wife and daughter.

The medical team had great difficulty in finding my veins. I was so swollen, and I later found out I was thirty-three kilograms heavier because of excess fluid than I was at my last appointment on the Monday before.

I can remember putting on the hair net and laughing about my "sexy" stockings.

Lauren, our beautiful midwife, was with me the whole way. She asked us what we wanted to happen with the baby once he or she was born. Did we want baby to stay with me the whole time or did we want him or her to go to the morgue? I wanted bubs to stay with me, even though I was going to be under a general anesthetic. Lauren kept this promise. She also took my phone into theatre so she could take photos of our precious angel as soon as he or she was born.

On Saturday, 22 November 2014 at 11:33 am, Ruby Gwen Margaret Williams was born sleeping. She weighed six pounds, ten ounces at thirty-six weeks and six days gestation. It was predicted she would have been around the ten-pound mark if I had gone full term.

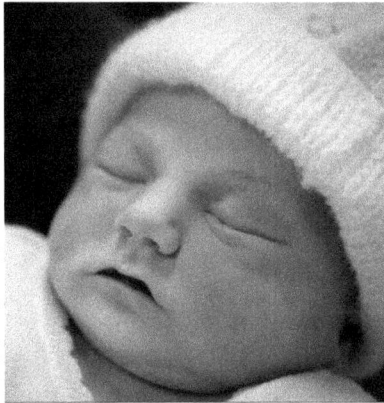

It wasn't until around 2:15pm that we got out of theatre and up to ICU and Kyle could see me and meet our brand new, sleeping, but so beautiful baby girl. Our Ruby girl.

As I was still waking up, Kyle introduced our daughter to everyone. Although we were both devastated, we were as proud as punch. It was like we put the fact that she was born sleeping aside for a second. We wanted to show our baby girl off to the whole world!
Our parents were the first ones to meet Ruby, followed by our brothers and sisters and our closest friends who are family anyway. We broke the record of visitors in an ICU room at once for the hospital: twenty-two people, all there for us and our daughter.

When I finally came to, I can remember Kyle handing Ruby

to me and saying, "We had a baby girl, Ruby, and she's beautiful. Would you like to hold her?" Of course I did. We both spent some time checking her out, over and over again. We were in total awe of what the two of us had made, all by ourselves. She was and still is perfect.

Kyle slept up in ICU with us, his girls, for two nights before we were moved to the maternity ward.

While still in ICU, we got to bathe Ruby, dress her, kiss her, cuddle her, one of our dearest friends read her a book, loads of photos were taken (I'm so happy everyone went snap happy). Impressionable Kids came in and did Ruby's hand and feet impressions. We cut a lock of her hair, her fuzzy wuzzy hair.

I can remember undressing her and having skin to skin time with her after Mum had given her a bath, and this was a beautiful time. I remember just rubbing her back and patting her little bottom. I knew she was gone and wasn't coming back, but it's just what came naturally and what I wanted to do.

It didn't seem too long before we were asked if we wanted an autopsy performed on Ruby. This meant that she would have to go to Melbourne and then she would be taken straight to the funeral directors until her funeral. We decided that we needed to send her on a road trip to Melbourne to have it done, for our peace of mind and for our future babies.

Ruby was with us in a cold cot, angel crib, cuddle cot, for two and a half days before she went to Melbourne. Again, I can only remember bits and pieces. I think it was my body and mind's way of protecting me. I was still fairly doped up and dopey on that Monday we said goodbye. I kissed our daughter goodbye and told her that I loved her so much and then handed her over to Kyle so Lauren, our midwife, could take her to the funeral director. It was so quiet after Ruby left.

The next few days, everyone concentrated on getting me better and healthy again. The doctors said that if I had left it until Saturday to get checked out, I probably wouldn't be here either. They would have been digging two graves.

It wasn't until the following Friday that things — Ruby — actually hit me. I was well enough for a big ugly dose of stupid reality to hit me fair and square in my heart. This was the beginning of me grieving the loss of my daughter. I cried all night, looked at my phone all night and listened to the baby across the hall cry, all night. The nurses on that night were awesome. One, in particular, sat with me until I fell asleep in the early hours of the morning; she really was wonderful. The next day; I asked if Kyle could stay that night. I needed him to be there with me. They said that it was not a problem at all. I was so relieved.

Not much sleep was got that night. We planned Ruby's whole funeral down to a tee. And we cried a lot, together. We looked at her photos and spoke to her as if she was still here on this earth with us. That night, although it sounds a little weird, was one of the most beautiful nights of my life, and a very important one.

Nine days after giving birth to our angel, I was released from hospital. I still had a lot of physical healing to do as my wound reopened after having the stitch taken out, so I had a vacuum dressing put on.

Our families, oh my god, our families were absolutely beautiful, amazing and supportive, and still are. I can remember Dad telling us not to worry about the funeral costs; whatever we wanted for our girl, we would get. That was such a relief.

The next couple of days were spent confirming the finer details of Ruby's funeral. Also, getting used to people looking at us differently and crossing the road just in front of us to avoid us. One of the biggest changes for me was the smell of our house. I hated it, and it took me some time before I could love our house and our home again.

Our beautiful first-born baby girl, Ruby, was buried on 5 December 2014. Her grave is right in front of my dearest Nan. We wanted them to be as close together as they could get. The day was beautiful, and everything happened just how we planned it.

My sister and Kyle's sister delivered Ruby's short but interesting eulogy, and our awesome friend read out a lovely poem. Both our fathers had one of the toughest jobs that day — they carried their granddaughter to her resting place.

Her flowers were bright and colourful and covered the top of her tiny casket. Caskets that size should never have to be made!

The best thing our friend said to us that day while she was hugging us was that we were to stay there for as long as we needed to; no one could tell us that it was time to go. I thank her so much for telling us that.

During my stay in hospital, our families were amazing. If Kyle wasn't with me, my mum was. My dear old Pop, he came and had tea with me every single night, such a pillar of support. Our friends were, and still are, amazing. They speak Ruby's name and talk about her as if she were here with us. They aren't afraid that they might upset us. We love them so much more for this.

So, now our little Miss Ruby is a year old. Her first birthday was a great day; we didn't want it to be sad, and we wanted to celebrate just as any other parents would with a living child. Our family and friends and our midwife all gathered for an early tea at Ruby's place (the cemetery) and of course, a big pink birthday cake. She got presents and cards and we sang happy birthday.

Ruby is also now a big sister. Miss Matilda Mary Lauren was born on 5 February 2016. She is a spitting image of her big sister, and we have no doubt that they have some sort of connection. Matilda and any other future siblings will grow up to know their big sister and how she has changed and made so many lives better. She has definitely done her job down here on earth.

If I could offer one bit of advice or guidance for those who are going through something similar, I would say do what you have to do, how you want to do it, and when it feels right for you to do it. No one else but you! And be gentle with yourself. Cry when you feel the need to and don't feel one ounce of guilt if you find yourself smiling. You're allowed to!

Annaleise & Kyle Williams

Oliver

I am mum to four children: three living, one not.

I have an eighteen-year-old daughter from my first marriage and three from my second marriage. All three from my second marriage are IVF miracle babies.

My first IVF pregnancy was amazing. At the time, my husband, Jim, and I were both Defence Force members, and as life throws you curveballs, we found I was going in for my first egg collection after he was being deployed to Afghanistan. So while everything was happening with me, he was busy depositing lots of sperm to be frozen. Looking back now, it was quite funny.

So off he went, and in I came to have my transfer. We had success on the second attempt, and plenty of eggs on ice too, which was great to know. Our little man arrived by inducement on Christmas Eve, 2009. His dad had arrived back in the country when I was seven months pregnant, which was hard to explain to those not in the know!

Even though I had now had two pregnancies, I also discovered I had a blood condition that caused me to clot. Not thinking this would impact on my ability to successfully deliver my baby, my IVF specialists monitored my delivery to a tee. I was in good hands, as was my baby boy.

After six months, we thought we should start trying again, as age was against me and I did not want to leave our run too late. Another round of transfers, this time more difficult, but then success again! I was amazed at how my body could do this a second time. I felt ready to smother another little one with love, and from the moment we knew I was pregnant, I had a feeling it was another boy. I even named him Oliver— although I never told anyone, including my husband.

Oliver was with me for just under eight weeks, nearly two months. We found out later it was my blood condition that had taken him from us, which was sad in a sense that maybe things could have been different. I had the curette on my birthday, seven days later. That gets me every year, as does the memory of the IVF doctor telling us we had lost.

Since the blood condition causes clotting, I have always had to have the Rhesus factor needle (given to mothers who have blood conditions or whose blood type might be incompatible with their baby's blood type) after birth as well; after finding out about our loss, the worst thing was having to trot down to the maternity ward at the hospital to have the needle. Cruel. I cried my eyes out that day, and have many times since.

The loss never leaves you. I wanted to remember our little one in some way that meant he was with us always. I had the ultrasound photo that was given to us and the pregnancy test indicator sewn into the belly of a teddy bear. That teddy sits in our room, up high. We have family stickers on our car— one sticker to represent every family member—and I got one for Oliver. It sits above the rest of us and has a halo to signify a lost baby. I don't care what people think; he was with us and he deserves to be thought of and seen.

Loss comes in so many ways, and grief takes us in so many ways. Since I've written this, I have lost my mum and have since found out after her passing that she gave birth to two sons I had no idea about. She died at age eighty-seven, and I am heartbroken that she could never talk of them with me.

I now work in an area of welfare within Defence, and part of my role is supporting parents who lose a son or daughter through their service. It does not matter what age a child is when they leave us; it always hurts, and the grief does not go away, which makes it even more important that we celebrate our babies' lives, even though they were so short. Babies are born out of our love and with love, and always will be.

Maree Grindrod

My name is Maree Grindrod. I am a fifty-one year-old mother and full time serving soldier. I am mum to three earth children, two step-children and one heavenly child. I work within welfare and as a mum who has lost, I wanted to share my story to help others understand there are many ways to grieve.

I would love to work within the IVF area of grief counseling as a social worker; doing my degree studies now by distance education.

Our Beautiful Boys
Our Little Lights

For Adam, Liam, Heath, Hayden, baby Ashen, & the angels we never met. Loving you all like the sunflowers love the sun.

As an adult, I had heard that there was an overwhelming euphoric feeling you experienced when you delivered a baby. Having had a difficult first pregnancy and complicated birth that ended in an emergency caesarean, I don't remember much of those first few hours or days, and it certainly wasn't the experience I had anticipated. But I have my son, Liam, who brings me joy each day and has been my strength during a difficult path to grow our family.

When I met my husband Adam, Liam was two years old, and Adam made a commitment to not only be by my side but Liam's as well. We knew we wanted more children and it wasn't long before we found out that I had fallen pregnant.

From that moment, our lives were changed forever; we were filled with so much joy and excitement when we found out we were expecting twins.

It was almost hard to believe that it was happening to us! Each time we got to see our baby boys growing together, it made us feel like we were doing something special. Liam kissed my tummy each night and said goodnight to his brothers. All seemed to make sense once Adam and I were expecting; we were meant to know each other and love our boys.

I was sitting in a chair when I felt an enormous kick from one of our babies. It wasn't long and I could feel my underwear was wet and as I tried to get up to get to the toilet, I could feel fluid gushing out. I tried to sit back down to make it stop but it wouldn't; my waters had broken early. I was at my mum's and I had family with me. I don't know how Adam drove me to the hospital, but he did, and my mum came too.

I kept saying, "Am I going to have to deliver these babies?" I knew it was too early. I could only hope that my waters hadn't broken and that I had, in fact, wet myself epically, like my three-year-old son at the time was sure I did.

I was terrified that night at the hospital, scared to move. Our babies were fraternal twins, so each was in a separate sac, but I knew I had lost fluid and I had to wait until the next morning to have an ultrasound to see just how much fluid and if our babies were okay. I had been to the hospital a week before with pains and had been sent home, being told it was probably just stretching, which often feels worse with twin pregnancies.

As I lay down and waited for the technician to start scanning, I kept thinking about the previous visit to the hospital and wished I knew what had gone so wrong. I had bleeding at nine weeks and my HCG levels had dropped and I was told then to go home and wait to miscarry. That never happened. When we had our first scan, the technician told us, "Yes, there are two sacs but at this stage, only one has a heartbeat, and the other is just a yolk sac. However, it's early, so when we scan again in two weeks, we will see, but expect that the other will absorb and be gone." That also didn't happen.

A lady came in and started scanning and showing us images of Twin A who had lost the fluid and I felt relief. We were okay. My heart sank when a man came in, seemingly annoyed with the lady scanning, and took over. He apologised said, "I'm sorry, but this foetus is gone." He asked if we needed a moment, but I couldn't speak.

He continued to say they would try and get me to carry to term as Twin B was growing well and everything looked great. He said when I delivered Twin B, expect that my body would dissolve the foetus of Twin A and what may be left I wouldn't want to see. He then proceeded to print a picture of Twin B and wished us well. I left that ultrasound picture on the printer. If I couldn't see my baby that had just died, it didn't feel right celebrating another.

I returned to the ward with my husband in disbelief at what we had just heard. I was in enormous pain and I couldn't figure out why. The pain kept coming and I realised I was having contractions and they were coming quick. I was about to deliver the baby that had died inside me that I could no longer feel.

I have searched for the memories of this birth over the past few years, but they come to me in moments and in dreams. I think it was so emotionally painful I've protected myself by blocking a lot of it out. I remember my strong husband and my brave mum being there and holding their own emotions back to support me through the birth.

When Twin A was born, he was born sleeping. I looked at

him and he was so precious, so much like his brother Liam, and I was so in love with our boy. I don't know why, but I hadn't considered that I would lose both.

When the contractions started again, I thought I was going to die. The fear I had at that moment was something I'd never experienced before. I knew Twin B was alive and healthy and my body was delivering him too soon. The pain of his waters breaking was significant of losing him ... it was happening again.

Twin B came into this world full of life and so much like both of his brothers and looking a lot like his dad. Arriving too early meant we could only hold him in our arms until he passed peacefully. The moment my boys were delivered, despite the tragic circumstances that surrounded their arrival, I experienced the overwhelming euphoric feeling that made me feel connected and enraptured to meet them. We named our sons Heath William Nix and Hayden Asher Nix.

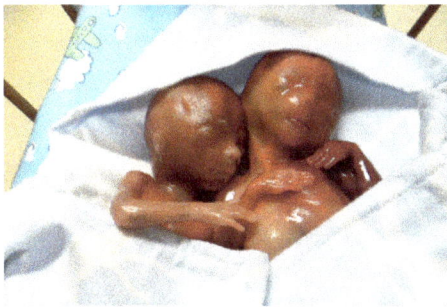

The time we got to spend with our boys was so intimate and special and I am so grateful for it. We were able to be able to hold them and take photos so we have lasting memories of our boys. I lay them in a small crib next to my bed as I lay in the delivery suite, listening to other newborn babies cry. I watched my two boys lay still next to me. I sang them "Twinkle, Twinkle Little Star" as I knew I would have sang it to them as they grew. I would always wonder what they would have been like as they had grown.

Adam and I looked at their features and admired the things about them that reminded us that they were our sons. We made plans for their service, and everything seemed very surreal. When we had to say goodbye, and we did so knowing we had got to know our boys and they would have known just how much we loved them.

Pregnancy is such an innate part of the human experience and occurs so frequently without complication. We hear all the announcements, reveals, and share the excitement with others, but we rarely hear the risks, the losses, the pain and the sadness that can be a part of someone's pregnancy or birth. The silence surrounding the difficulty of pregnancy and birth can make it even more complicated when you experience it because there is very little understanding from others.

The grief I experienced was exceptionally difficult to navigate because it was unlike anything I have experienced in my life. I couldn't understand what was wrong with me, and the grief scared me because it was all part of my healing, but to heal, I had to face the pain. Finding forgiveness for myself and others and understanding my husband's grief as he was grieving differently than me were all necessary for me to accept what had happened but to also heal from the pain.

In our time to try and grow our family, I have had such difficulty with the way the sad news is delivered. I understand medical professionals see this every day and to them, it's a foetus. For us, it's a baby, a baby we loved from the moment we knew we had fallen pregnant. We have experienced multiple losses outside of our twin pregnancy, and the most difficult thing aside from our grief for me has been the medical process you have to endure to be able to grow your family. I found more empathy from the receptionist taking my payment for an ultrasound than I did from the fertility specialist delivering the difficult news.

The grief I experienced when we lost our boys made everything so small and the pain so large. It almost seemed as though our world stopped in that moment whilst everything around us kept moving. I had difficulty seeing babies for quite some time and I think it was purely a reminder of what we had lost that made it so hard. I was angry at myself for not knowing that there was something wrong. Even though the early labour was brought on by an infection in Twin A's amniotic sac that went undetected by my GP, hospital, and emergency staff, I still felt I had let it happen. I had guilt and blame, and I was angry at the way things happened.

I now know what happened was not my fault and was just unlucky that it happened to us, but we did everything during that pregnancy to care for our babies. It just wasn't something we could have changed. I am also aware now that all that emotion I felt during that time and years to come was normal too. I was grieving the loss of our boys. I can still feel the rawness of that time momentarily and at times, I want to because it brings me close to them.

Life is rolling on

Each day has passed before I've had a chance to decide what I want
to do
I am stuck somewhere between feeling okay and my world is falling
apart
No one could have prepared me for this
Nobody could prepare themselves for this
Craving normality, I am disconnected, feared and forgotten
You don't know what to say to me, so you say nothing at all
Your fear of death
Your fear of grief
Not mine
I am reminded I am being so strong
Don't be silly, I have no choice
I had to face that my baby boys were dying
I had to accept that they had died
I had to acknowledge the short life they had
Let me speak about my babies I gave birth to
Let it be okay for me to grieve for them
Don't make me protect you from them
Understand that I am changed because of this
Understand that I will never be that person again

Our sons came into this world too soon to live with us, but
they are with us in each thing we do and guide us in so
many ways through life. I remember coming home from the
hospital and crying in the shower over the loss of our boys.
Then this moment of calmness came over me, like a big warm
hug, and I remember looking up at the bathroom ceiling and
saying, "Thank you." At that very moment, I knew my boys
were with me and that gave me something to believe in. Not
in a religious sense, but in a spiritual one. That connection I
felt to our boys was so strong I had to believe in it.

This year, it has been five years since Heath and Hayden

were born. They have taught me so many things about my-self, the world, and the people around me that I can only be grateful for the love I have for them. When Adam and I got married, we wanted to have children, and we joked about having a large family. Adam and I are now foster carers and we couldn't imagine our life any other way. I reached a point in the process to have a baby that I simply could not keep going and experience any more losses.

We knew there was a need for safe, loving homes for children who had experienced trauma and the loss and grief of being separated from their families. We had lots of love to give. Liam longed for a baby brother or sister, but we also felt drawn to help foster children and their families who, because of our own experience of the loss of our children, we felt such empathy and an understanding of their grief.

We currently have a full house of little boys, including twins, filled with mess, noise, laughter, tears, joy, wee all over the bathroom, and lots of love.
My beautiful boys, Heath and Hayden, I know you lead us

Danielle Nix

Danielle has always had a passion for writing and a desire to create and perform. Her creativity led her to become a dance teacher at a young age and it was through teaching her love of children grew. Danielle knew she always wanted to be a mum and she dreamt of large families, big meals and messy fun.

The expectation Danielle had of pregnancy and motherhood left her in anguish when she experienced multiple losses trying to grow her family. Danielle is married to her husband Adam who is an amazing father to all their children, a mum to her roaring dinosaur son Liam, mum to Heath, Hayden, and baby Ashen, her angel babies, and foster mum to four spirited sons.

Writing has been an opportunity to explore the grief experienced after loss and she is honoured to share her story with others.

Janice Dufficy

Volunteer For Angel Gowns Australia

At the outset, I would like to acknowledge the pain you have and will continue to experience, following the tragic loss of your four babies. I can only imagine your suffering and offer you my support.

As a mother myself, I know that when you realise you are pregnant, you fantasise about the sex of the baby, the hopes and anticipation of what this new life will mean, and the joy of bringing a life into the world to be loved and cherished by you, your husband, family, and friends. For you to have experienced four losses is beyond my comprehension.

Luckily for me, I had two uneventful, lovely pregnancies and ended up with two healthy children—my daughter, Leah (34), and son, Tom (30). I had the bonus of having, and still have, a wonderful husband, Terry, (forty years together in 2018) who is loving and supportive of my voluntary work and life adventures, and we have a wonderful extended family.

However, around four years ago, my son Tom took seriously ill and was urgently admitted to St. George Hospital where he was diagnosed with Aplastic Anaemia. I was then faced with the fact that I could lose my baby boy, who was now an adult. Luckily, as I write this piece, he's doing fine and on no medication, but it will be a lifelong battle.

As you would like this piece to concentrate on the voluntary aspects of my life, may I start by sharing some of the voluntary roles I've had over my life and my commitment to join Angel Gowns Australia as a volunteer seamstress.

Casting my mind back, I think my voluntary roles started when I was a Sunday school teacher at the age of fourteen at St. David's Church of England Church in Greenacre. Finishing school, I worked and following the birth of my daughter and not working full-time, I undertook the following voluntary roles during my children's formative years. They are:

- On the church cleaning roster for Menai Uniting Church
- Day leader for Playgroup
- Secretary of Menai Occasional Child Care Centre (over five years)
- Various activities at Menai Primary School: tutor reading program, canteen, covering many library books, etc
- At Menai Hawks Soccer Club, I was manager over the years of various teams and took on the role of Canteen Co-ordinator at one of the three fields operated by the Club—namely Casuarina Oval (over eight years)
- And any other duties as required!

Most recently, following a request I viewed on Facebook from Sutherland Shire Careers' Support Service, I am now assisting a disabled young man do his voluntary work at Sutherland Shire Council. I have been undertaking this role for approximately two years now, supporting this wonderful young man, and look forward to continuing this well into the future.

It may be interesting to learn that when I discovered who this young man was, he was someone special who I knew well. I first met him and his mother when I had my daughter, Leah, thirty-four years ago in St. George Hospital. We were both in the same hospital after giving birth to our first child. Both children went to the same playgroup, primary school, and were on the same soccer team!

When Leah married her partner, Amanda, in Portugal in 2013, they then went down the path of donor sperm from the USA to conceive a child. It was successful and little Luke was born on 16 April 2014. My boss at the time gave me the day off, and as a new grandmother, I received flowers for doing nothing—Amanda did all the hard work! How nice! This was followed by the eagerly awaited birth of his biological brother, Conor, on 1 December 2016.

Prior to the birth of Luke (my first grandchild), I embarked on my crocheting passion, making heaps of unusual things in anticipation of Luke's arrival and posting photos of my creations on Facebook.

Over lunch with long-time friends who had seen my creations, a very good friend of mine, Kerrie Jones, suggested that I make contact with a new organisation known as Angel Gowns Australia (AGA), thinking that they may want me to make crocheted items for them. I pursued this via email and received a reply stating that crocheting wasn't required, but seamstresses were.

I thought about this for a while as I hadn't sewn for a few years, and didn't know whether my old Janome machine could be resurrected or function without encouragement, and I had reservations about my ability. My faithful Janome is still behaving, and my dining room has been taken over with my sewing for AGA.

I am not a professional sewer but have always loved sewing given the time. I have recovered lounges, drafted patterns, sewn beautiful dresses in my younger days, made curtains, embroidered, and more. I did rather well in year ten quite a few decades ago, and my School Certificate results put me in the top ten percent of New South Wales.

After thinking about this new commitment, I decided to give it a go. I filled in the necessary forms, submitted my sample gowns, and lo and behold, I was accepted! My phone rang hot as I posted this on my Facebook page and couldn't wait to get started.

I will never forget receiving my first wedding gown to work on when I attended an open day at Engadine Community Centre in January 2015. I burst through the front door when I arrived home, full of enthusiasm to show my husband. I then spent hours thinking of what I was going to do with it, particularly when I realised how special this gown was to the bride on her wedding day and how important her donation was.

When putting the scissors and making my first cut on the gown, the significance of my commitment to AGA became very real and confronting. I had to go to my very best, be creative, and make garments symbolic of the wedding gown for our little Angels. However, this can be difficult as depending on the gown; you are sometimes limited.

Also, our clientele—Hospitals Australia-wide—have requested that our gowns be simple and unisex when possible. As most of the gowns donated lend themselves to feminine creations, I have tried to focus on male garments.

With my first gown, I knew the name and details of the donor. The first thing I made was a keepsake for the bride, incorporating a design that was symbolic of her gown. The photograph below shows the heart cushion I made, depicting the lace over the satin, and then using the gathered lace from her train, I surrounded the heart with it. I then posted it off with a note of thanks to the bride with my details and shortly thereafter received a wonderful personal phone call thanking me and advising she had been in touch with her relatives following receipt of her keepsake.

Due to the number of donated gowns AGA currently has ready for transformation and our privacy laws, we no longer provide keepsakes, unfortunately.

This photo depicts the heart keepsake I made for the donor bride, a sleeping bag with vest, bonnet and wrap.

On reflecting upon my past, I realise where my need and desire to join AGA arose. Both my grandmothers and my mother lost little girls. My grandmother, Ethel Maud Ingle-Olson (Brady), lost Beryl at two years of age, my other grandmother, Gwendoline Maud Mafeking Johnston (Marshall), lost Anne at nine months, and my mother, Enid Gwendoline Ingle-Olson (Johnston), lost my sister Jill at three weeks and also found her sister Anne "asleep" when she was a young girl.

All the above-bereaved mothers were told to "just get on with it" and forgot their loss. It was never acknowledged or discussed and they endured their grief silently, constantly, and sadly. My wonderful Mum, now ninety, recently cried yet again, when I asked her about their losses. Mum loves what I do for AGA and acknowledges this, but says that she wishes I was doing something for the living. She, at ninety, doesn't realise that our Angels are still living—in our hearts always. Mum still thinks differently and still suffers her loss as if it was yesterday. I love Mum dearly. She says the truth and is incredibly honest, loving, and supportive.

Thank goodness for AGA. Angel Gowns Australia has given me, as a volunteer, purpose, love, support, enduring friendships, and the opportunity to spend my time doing something voluntary for a community who sadly needs this service. As a volunteer over many years and genres, I have unexpectedly received benefits that I had no idea I would experience. Longstanding friendship is a very special one, an acknowledgement (sometimes unexpectedly), and huge personal satisfaction that my efforts have, in some way, maybe made a difference.

On a silly note, I went to the hairdresser recently and was talking about my wonderful adventures. My hairdresser said that she has wealthy friends who are bored. Well, why aren't they volunteering? They surely have the opportunity and talent to do something for others, so why don't they embark on a new wonderful journey and experience the satisfaction of giving whatever time they can spare in one of the many facets of volunteering to suit their ability and interest? They would be welcomed with open arms.

As an amateur seamstress, sewing is what I try to do to the best of my ability. AGA members don't see one another regularly, but when we do get together, the camaraderie, advice, and sharing of ideas is an unexpected and welcome benefit. As an added bonus, sewing isn't all that is involved when you become involved with AGA. Many AGA volunteers don't know one another personally, but there are opportunities to assist in other ways and finally meet up with AGA Facebook friends.

I have had the privilege of being part of working bees at Linnwood House, Guildford on various occasions, a packing day at Ryde, and manning information stalls at craft shows at Rosehill, Homebush, Darling Harbour, and Glebe Island, and look forward to more. We've also had sewing bee weekends away and I've attended two at Neville Siding and one on the Central Coast.

I seem to be a magnet for strange questions/people, and when at Glebe Island, a lady came up to me to ask whether AGA would consider making Angel garments for pets! I spoke to her sympathetically, and I think I referred her to Pets at Peace.

Janice Dufficy

I worked for Members of Parliament in NSW for decades, the last member being Linda Burney in her electorate office, finishing in August 2015.

I'm a keen Jazzerciser (over thirty-five years). I play golf with the Alfords Point Ladies Social Club (fifteen years), but I'm hopeless at it; however, one good shot out of eighteen holes ensures my return.

I obtained a Graduate Certificate in Multicultural Journalism at the University of Wollongong at around fifty years of age, proving you are never too old to learn.
I'm also a Justice of the Peace.

Jayden James

Before I begin my story, I'd like to start by mentioning my two sisters who have both experienced pregnancy complications and miscarriage, including the coordinator of this book, Melissa. I admire and respect her for giving the women who have generously opened their hearts to contribute to this book the chance to express themselves and to hopefully feel some sort of closure in sharing these beautiful and inspiring stories.

Although I have not experienced the loss of a pregnancy, I have known the difficult feelings and the emotional roller coaster associated with premature childbirth. Experiencing my sister's heartbreak of miscarriage and stillbirth and trying to comfort and support her when not knowing what to do … then there were feelings of anticipation and worry when my twin sister also experienced premature labour not long after I did. Not knowing what the outcome will be is quite daunting.

My husband and I had been in a relationship for over five years before we married. We decided to try to start a family soon after our wedding. In the first month of trying, a positive test result came up on a home pregnancy test. I had a few symptoms so I went to the doctors for a blood test. Hormone levels were low at twenty-two, so the doctor advised me to do another test within forty-eight hours and it dropped to ten.

Within the week, I had an extremely horrible and painful period, which is unusual for me. The doctor explained that I might have had a very early miscarriage. I felt quite disappointed and was confused about what had happened.

We tried the next two months with no positive results. By the third month, I fell pregnant with all the signs and symptoms and a strong hormone level. Pregnancy was well on its way with all of the expected appointments with my obstetrician.

Morning sickness set in until sixteen weeks. Cravings of heavy food like pasta and burgers became normal for me. Although I was growing, my belly wasn't growing as big as the usual size at each gestational period.

At thirty-one weeks, my obstetrician noticed no change in growth from my twenty-eight-week check-up. He seemed concerned and requested an extra scan done by another specialist to measure the baby's growth. Of course, I felt very nervous and scared: would my baby be okay? My obstetrician booked me in to have several check-ups at the hospital to monitor the baby's heart rate. He wanted me to have steroid injections to prepare the baby's lungs in case of an early delivery. I did this for the next two weeks. He told us our baby had stopped growing at twenty-eight-weeks.

By the thirty-third week of my pregnancy, I was beginning to have Braxton Hicks contractions. I went to the hospital for my usual check-up that afternoon. The nurses set me up and kept checking the baby's heart rate. I asked if everything was okay, as the heart seemed very low. I was beginning to understand how these machines worked so I was concerned. The nurse explained that I was actually having contractions and the baby seemed a little bit stressed. They called the obstetrician and he ordered another steroid shot and asked me to stay overnight for observation. I knew something was not right by this stage. I called my husband and he stayed the night with me. I didn't get any sleep as I was attached to monitors all night.

The next morning at 7am, I received a phone call from our obstetrician. He explained to me that sometimes in situations like mine, the placenta decides to die prematurely. He said that sometimes it's safer to take the baby out earlier rather than keeping the baby inside the womb where it was not being fed and growing properly. He told us that we were going to be parents that morning!

A midwife came to speak to us about the possibilities of our child not surviving. I had hope and I knew that my baby was going to be okay.

My husband and I were excited but so scared at the same time. We both had no idea what to expect. Our emotions were everywhere! We questioned every moment; was our baby going to be all right mentally and physically? Did I let our baby down by not nourishing our baby properly? I had done everything by the book when it came to my pregnancy.

At 8.30am on 23rd August 2007, I was given a spinal block and our beautiful son, Jayden James, was born by emergency Caesarian. All I wanted to hear was his first cry. When he let out a loud scream, I felt such relief. But Jayden was born very tiny; he weighed one point three kilograms. He was so tiny and so precious.

He could breathe on his own, but he was just too small to be out of the Special Care Nursery. He needed to grow, and he slept in the humid crib for three weeks. He was tube fed my breast milk. I was nicknamed "Daisy" in the NICU because I had an almost endless supply of milk! I guess it was meant to be because my beautiful boy needed as much nourishment as he could get.

Each day, he improved with a few little scares along the way. I was so proud. We were so proud.

The nurses had let me stay in hospital for five days so I could bond with him while I was recovering. When the day came for me to have to leave Jayden at the hospital, I was a wreck. I wasn't supposed to go home without him. It was an unsettling feeling. I broke down and cried. But then I realised he would be in his own cot in our home before too long. We had to be patient.

I visited him every day, being dropped off and picked up while still recovering from the caesarian section. Funnily enough, I forgot about the pain I was in. I was just focused on getting our boy home. I was in my own world. I felt like the only people in my world were my son and I. I didn't realise this until he was home. A mother's instinct, I guess. Although I had the support of my husband and family, my main focus was Jayden.

After a long three weeks, Jayden was allowed to sleep in a cot, still in the NICU. We were so happy! He was putting on weight and getting stronger. Another week in the NICU and he was allowed to come home! Finally! This was one of our happiest moments.

I am so blessed that we were given such a precious miracle in our life. Jayden is now nine years old, and he is a wonderful child. These hard times were also an amazing learning time for us. They made us stronger and helped us appreciate life so much more.

I respect each and every one of the women who has contributed to this book, for sharing your stories. Writing and sharing can be good ways to find closure. And to the precious Angels that are not with us on earth, you will always be in our hearts.

Rebecca Riggio

My name is Rebecca. I am thirty-five years old. I live in Sydney NSW and grew up on acreage which makes me love nature and open surroundings.

Melissa Desveaux is my older sister. I am an identical twin, and I have a younger brother. I became a hairdresser at the age of fifteen years old and I still love my career to this day. I run a small home salon and it's something I enjoy doing every day.

I married my husband Mark when I was twenty-three. We have two children, Jayden now eleven years old and Sienna, now nine years old. My family is my life and I wouldn't have it any other way!

I would like to take this opportunity to thank my sister, Melissa Desveaux, for all the hard work and dedication she has put into *Comfort for Tears* and giving other people the opportunity to share their personal and amazing stories throughout pregnancy and loss. I am proud of my sister and so honoured to be a part of this amazing book.

Our Alexander the Great

I loved being pregnant. I've wanted to be a mummy since I was a child … I found out I was pregnant in March 2018 with my first baby. My husband and I were so very excited. At thirteen weeks, our baby was very healthy and a day in front with growth.

At twenty weeks, it was a very different story. They found that the baby was twelve days behind and the amniotic fluid was low. I was now high risk and changed hospitals.

After a few more scans and several more weeks, the doctors diagnosed our baby with Intrauterine Growth Restriction (IUGR). I was now to be heavily monitored and was warned of the possibility of stillbirth.

Thursday, August 2nd, 2018 started like any other day. My husband, Peter, had taken the morning off to take me to my eighth ultrasound. We went to VicRoads to renew my licence; I was coming off my P plates, so a new photo was needed.

We arrived at Monash Hospital as we had done for the last four weeks. This ultrasound was to see the blood flow between the placenta and bub. We didn't wait long before a midwife called my name. When we got to the room, she asked if I had felt movement.

"Yes," I said, "but he's quiet in the mornings."

She put the Doppler on my tummy. There he was, our perfect bub, facing us. He's still. WHY is he still? I was thinking. Then she said it. The words I wish no one should ever have to hear.

"I'm so sorry to have to be the one to tell you this, but I think your baby has died."

There he was on the screen; no movement, no heartbeat, no … NOTHING!

I went into total meltdown. WHY ME? WHY Peter? I started hyperventilating. Pete went bright red. Catherine told us she had to get another midwife to confirm. She came straight back as she didn't want us left alone.

I cried and couldn't stop. I remember asking my midwife if she was okay. She said she was and not to worry about her. I do it all the time, and even asked everybody who looked after me in the coming days. The second midwife came in to confirm. Again, we saw our precious bub on that screen. It's something I think about every day. It just broke us.

They quickly got us into a birthing suite, far away from the other rooms. It is used especially for mummies like me. We had new midwives come in to look after me and explained what was to happen. She asked us if we had a name. We did.

"Alexander," I said. I was so very proud of him, our precious little boy.
I begged for a Caesarean, but they wouldn't give me one. She didn't go into full details but said they don't because it can

make chances of having another baby difficult as they would have to cut down my tummy, not across, which can damage my uterus.

She then explained that they would induce me via tablets. She said we could stay there for as long as we wanted after he was born and do all the things like cuddle him, kiss him, have him in the room with us overnight, take photos, bathe and dress him. All the things we would have done normally.

While they were waiting for the doctors to come and talk about the next steps, I asked, "How can this be? I can still feel him moving inside me." My midwife said it's the waters that move the bub around. I felt so very sick and extremely sad at knowing that.

We waited and waited for the doctors to come in. Unfortunately, they wouldn't be coming until later that night as they had emergencies that day. After an hour and a half, maybe two hours, I wanted my parents badly so that we made the phone calls neither of us will forget.

I'm crying as I write this…

Mum asked me how we went; she sounded hopeful and excited. I broke down and said, "My baby died, Mum. I have to give birth to him."

"Naomi, oh Naomi!" and mum broke down too. She asked who I wanted her to call. I left it up to her as I couldn't.

They told us to come back a bit later, so we decided to leave hospital, go home, and pack a bag. On the way home, Peter told me he wanted to change our son's middle name so he'd have something of Peter too. His name was then Alexander Peter.

On the way back to the hospital, Mum called. She had told

my dad, brother, and sister-in-law. They met us at the hospital with my other sister-in-law (who is Pete's sister; I have a few sisters-in-law).

We didn't wait too long before the doctors came in and explained what was going to happen. The first tablet I had to take that night would to take thirty-six hours to take effect in order to get my body ready for labour and birth. The next one would be inserted into my cervix when I came back on Saturday. After that, I would have one tablet every four hours for a twelve hour period. If it didn't work, they would give my body a rest for twelve to twenty-four hours before starting the process again.

Taking that first tablet was the worst thing. I felt like I was ending my pregnancy and I really wasn't ready for that. I was still feeling Alexander "moving" inside my body. With my darling husband on one side, Dad on the other, and everyone else behind me and crying with me, I took that bloody tablet that started the process. I was twenty-five weeks and five days. Our darling little fighter had passed away.

Friday came, and so did my parents, best friend, Peter's sisters, my brother- and sister-in-law. I wasn't left alone.

"Do everything you think you might regret later," I was told.

So I took my last pregnancy photo that day, the last photo of Alexander and me together before he was born.

We had bought Alexander a Mickey Mouse security blanket weeks before, and I came up with this idea: I tucked it into my top, slept with it, etc. Peter did the same so that Alexander would have my/our scent with him forever. I asked Mum and Dad to buy me another if they could. They did. When Alexander was born, that one was with him all the time in the cot, and we have photos of him with it too. When it was time for us to part ways, I gave the blanket I was holding onto to him (which was wrapped up with him and never left) and I took his so that we would have a piece of each other forever.

My OB called me that Friday; she had looked after me before I became high risk at my previous hospital. She was able to get me a bed. I was so very grateful to her for this and will be forever.

Saturday came, and I could not move out of bed! My best friend was taking us to the hospital that morning. But Peter couldn't get me up. She arrived while I was still laying there. It took maybe another half hour to hour to get up. Peter got me into doing a step system. First was getting out of bed and having a shower. He packed while I did that. I was ready for hospital...

We don't live far away, but that drive seemed like hours. I cried the whole way there. I didn't want this to happen. It felt like a dream.

We arrived and Peter ran up to the maternity ward to let them know I was coming. Pete's sister met us halfway and together, the three of them managed to get me to reception. As soon as they saw me, I had midwives running to me from all different directions. I froze.

This isn't real; this isn't happening to me. I can't do this, kept racing through my head.

I froze again. I could see a happy couple with their newborn baby up ahead and I would have to walk past them. I didn't though. They were ushered back into their room so I could walk past.

They finally got me into the room. It was set away from other birthing suites. Before you walk in, it had a set of double doors and a tiny little hallway with two rooms. They were both ours. One was for me, and the other had a cold cot, cuddle cot, and loads of information about the next steps.

Saturday was full on. I cried and cried. Our families came and sat with us for hours. A social worker came in to talk about what would happen next; plans we needed to make, plans for his funeral. They explained that we could get professional photos from an organisation called Heartfelt. A volunteer photographer would come in and take some photos if we wanted. "Yes, definitely!" we said.

My OB that was looking after me that day came in. Again, she went into detail about what the tablets did. It may take days for the baby to arrive, I was told. I was asked if I wanted to have any tests done on me or Alexander. I said yes to the bloods on me, and Alexander had a swab of his mouth and a skin biopsy from under his arm. Then I was asked if I wanted an autopsy done on him.

"WHAT? WHY?"

I completely broke down again. We decided not to have an autopsy done. He was too fragile and the doctors were pretty confident that he'd passed away of growth restriction.

Not long after that, I was given my first tablet. It had to be inserted into my cervix to dissolve. After that, I was given a tablet that had to dissolve under my tongue every four hours. Night came, and my dad stayed with Peter and me Saturday night. We thought he would be born; he wasn't. The first twelve hours came and went and still no baby. I was checked Sunday morning and the tablet hadn't dissolved. My OB wasn't worried, but I think my midwife was a little shocked.

We now had to wait twenty-four hours to start the tablets again. My body needed the rest, they said. I could still have my baby in that time, so I had to stay in hospital. By this time, I was on morphine and Valium to keep me calm. I didn't press for the morphine much as I didn't need it.

We had some of our siblings come in again with my parents on Sunday. They made me homemade food and brought coffee to us. I'll forever be thankful to them for that. Sunday night came and still no baby. It was just Pete and me that night.

Monday morning came, and we started the process all over again. The tablet was again inserted into my cervix. That day, we had my parents and brother with us, as well as friends popping in and out.

Monday night came and so did my labour at around 6pm. We had dinner, and more friends came in. Around 7 or 7:30, my waters broke. Shift change happened around 9pm. I needed to go to the bathroom so my midwife helped me. It wasn't anything I'd felt before' lots of pressure on my bladder. I was labouring in the front and my pains felt like intense period pain. I said I thought he was coming...

By that time, Peter's sisters had arrived and my parents were there. Everyone was ushered into the next room while I was examined. It was just Peter and my midwives. Yes, it was time; he was coming and I was not ready.

My active labour (pushing) was an extremely slow process and lasted four and a half hours. He was born breech with his bottom up in the air, mooning everyone with his legs crossed over. His arms were also up above his head. The midwives couldn't pull on his body as he was so tiny and fragile. It was very much in his own time. His arms came out one at a time. All anyone could do was wait and guide him.

Our darling Alexander Peter was born Tuesday the 7th, August 2018 at 1:30am, weighing a tiny three hundred and forty grams and twenty-four centimeters long. I was twenty-six weeks and three days. I had a look at him, and he was wrapped and handed to Daddy for cuddles.

It was very quiet in the room just after he came out. It was so very sad and heartbreaking. There was a part of me that expected him to cry because that's what happens, babies cry. Mine didn't. My heart was shattered into a thousand pieces. My pregnancy had ended long before I was ready.

It wasn't long before the placenta came. I was impatient and uncomfortable by that time and again needed the bathroom. The midwives had put a small bowl in the toilet days before for "just in case." As soon as I sat down, the placenta fell out. I will spare you the details. But right there and then, I could see what the doctors could see … it looked horrible and very tiny.

I showered and changed while Daddy and son had cuddles. This is when I saw him properly. He was so beautiful and I loved him instantly. I understand now what Mama's say about instant love and bonding when they see their babies for the first time. It was beautiful seeing him in his daddy's arms. I made the decision not to have cuddles as I was still feeling the medications. The midwives took him away to be cleaned and dressed and have his tests taken and I was seen by my OB.

It was a few hours before he was brought back to us. In that time, our family came in. To my surprise, Peter's brother had come not long after I'd started giving birth.

We were very lucky to have so very many cuddles and kisses with our boy. He was the spitting image of his daddy. He would have had his dark hair but my blonde eyebrows. He also had my flat feet. We were very lucky to have him in our room with us on Tuesday night, and Wednesday morning we had a naming ceremony and very beautiful photos taken by Heartfelt.

I was looking at his hand and footprints while planning his funeral and I noticed in his handprint, there was an image of a butterfly.

We held his funeral a week later. I didn't want people to wear black, just lots of colours. All our friends and family came and gave Alexander small gifts to go with him. We had him cremated, and he now has a very special shelf with teddy bears and photos on it. He is in his teddy bear urn.

I want to thank everyone who looked after me in those days and after, our friends and families for everything they did for us and for being there with us. We love them for that.

Most importantly, my husband, Peter. I love you so much, darling. Thank you for giving me strength each day.

To our Alexander,
We love you so very much, baby. We are so very proud of your strength and the fight you gave to stay with us. Forever our angel. Forever missed.

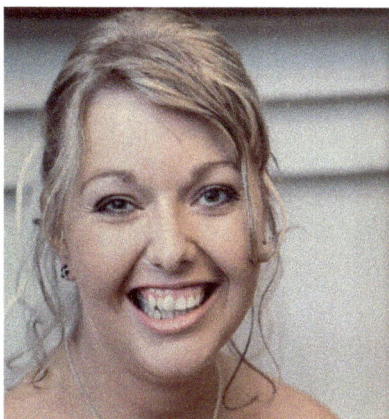

Naomi Carpinteri

Naomi Carpinteri is a mum of one. Married and lives in Melbourne.

She has experienced stillbirth. She now writes a blog about her life after her loss called *Alexander's Butterfly*.

Seven Angels...
Sette Angeli

I am the mother of seven Angels in heaven and ten
Earth Angels (eight beautiful boys and two gorgeous girls!)

My journey as a mother began in 1988 when I delivered
a healthy son. Two years later, in 1990, his brother would
follow. The following year, I had my first miscarriage, but I
didn't know it at the time. It was only in falling very ill and
having a cyst rupture on my ovary just shortly after that an
infection was discovered in my uterus caused by an incomplete miscarriage. It seemed like the loss of Baby Gabriel was
the beginning of something. I was in the midst of a bitter and
messy marriage breakup and not sure how to feel about this
loss. I wanted to grieve, but I found it so hard to cry for a
baby I didn't even know I was having. It would be years later
that I would be able to honour that loss and the space he/she
left in my life.

In 1994, I would be blessed with another son, and two years
later, I would endure another miscarriage—this time at
sixteen weeks. I was in Adelaide, and away from my other
children who I was missing desperately. I was unable to fly
and heartbroken to miss my second-born son's sixth birthday.
I had started to bleed and was sent for an ultrasound that
detected no heartbeat and a foetus too small for dates.

The sonographer quizzed me, asking, "Could you have miscarried and fallen pregnant again?"

I had no idea why she was asking or what this could mean.

I told her that that wasn't possible and she simply blurted out, "I had a woman in here just before you who is ten weeks pregnant and her baby is much bigger than yours."

I was mortified. How could she be so cruel? I continued to bleed, and that was that. I was sent in for a D&C, four days after the ultrasound—the waiting was hard, and yet part of me didn't want it to be over; I didn't want to say goodbye, I wasn't ready.

The hospital staff put me in the maternity wing, and I had to endure listening to the newborns cry while I waited to be taken to surgery. It was torture—a cruel and unusual punishment for a grieving mother to endure. A young mum walked past carrying her baby, and I couldn't help but stare as she walked away. My dream was shattered, but she held her dream in her arms. Life can be so unfair!

Broken, I headed to the beach and stood atop a cliff, icy wind whipping my hair, staring at the aqua ocean eroding the surface rock, feeling like grief was eroding my heart. I didn't know what to do with all of that sadness. I gave my baby the name Aspen Lee, and that day, laid her to rest in my mind on the coastline of South Australia. Primal sobs escaped my heart all the way home in the car. Then I poured all of the pain into a journal, into poetry, and into writing for the now-defunct grief newsletter *Pen Parents of Australia – Candlelight Magazine*. For seven years I worked tirelessly with them to counsel other grieving parents, to share my story and my poetry. Little did I know, rough times were not over for me yet.

I was blessed in 1997 to welcome a daughter and another son two years after her (1999) and eighteen months later, another daughter (in 2000). But in my quest to have more children, there would be more losses—in 2002 a miscarriage (Willow), then another baby boy born in 2003, another son arrived in 2004, and then three miscarriages followed consecutively in one year (Ash, Jael, & Rowan).

In October 2005, I was admitted to hospital for yet another D&C. My body wasn't giving this baby up. The hardest part of this one had been that my baby had a heartbeat, but it was too small for dates. My OBGYN counseled me to make a decision—if nature wasn't going to run its course, or if my body wasn't going to relinquish and expel this baby, then I needed to abort. I went to the Sunshine Coast for the week-end and prayed that I wouldn't have to make that decision, that I would be spared that agony, and thankfully, I was. By the time I returned for a follow-up ultrasound, there was no heartbeat. The decision was made.

After that, my OBGYN wrote to my GP and said, "Meekehleh's baby-making career is over!" So hurt and dis-gusted by the way he chose to word my desire to have a family, I called him and complained bitterly. He told me that although I was not yet forty, my body was acting like it was and I wasn't likely to ever have another healthy baby. I knew that I could prove him wrong.

In 2007 when I was delivered of another healthy son, I sent that OBGYN a birth announcement with a note: "Here's the healthy baby you said I'd never have!" My ninth child, and my first ever C-section. There and then, I came to the conclu-sion that I was done. I had managed it. I was blessed. I was grateful. I could breathe out. My family was complete!

All of those miscarriages had taken their toll. I was mentally and emotionally exhausted and knew that I could not do it all again. I was at university and beginning a new journey in my life—studying nursing so that I could become a midwife and support other women who, like me, had struggled through the milestones of pregnancy. I understood that overpowering urge to become a mother against all odds.

Once more, I changed my mind, and again I went on a quest

to add to my family. Unfortunately, in 2009 I lost yet another baby (Sam). I was beyond shattered and had to deal with yet another incompetent sonographer with zero compassion.

How can they say lightning doesn't strike twice in the same place? That's just not a legitimate quote; at least, it isn't for me. But now I was obsessed with wanting another child. I was yearning, and I wanted to fulfill that need. For several months I was denied the result I so desperately wanted, so I decided that if the test was negative one more time, I was giving up.

That month, the test was blessedly positive with exactly the same due date as the baby I lost in 2009 (Feb 25), and we had a road trip planned from Brisbane to Sydney with six children in tow. I hoped all would be well and I clung to a thin veil of hope. Two days after we arrived in New South Wales, I started spotting and decided that was that; there would be no more babies for me. I was done. I figured Heaven was proving to me that there was no more joy here for me.

To my surprise, the pregnancy continued, but not without drama. I was hospitalized from thirty-one weeks for bed rest because I was dilating and they feared an imminent arrival. And then my baby's heart rate was flat. He just didn't seem to be doing well inside. I was induced two weeks early and thankfully was able to have a VBAC, despite being in a high-risk category. I had a wonderful staff, and I was really looked after well. But my little boy's heart rate was still not satisfactory, and I saw the worried look on the doctor's face. He told me all I needed to know. It seemed like this wasn't to be my happily ever after at all. However, my tenth child arrived on the tenth of the month, thirteen and a half hours after I was induced. He was healthy and well. I had done it!

But by the time he was one month old, he had fallen very ill and would remain so until just before his first birthday. I nursed him back to health, after enduring one of the worst years of my entire life. He is now five and has just started school. He is perfect and beautiful and amazing, as are all my children.

Despite these trials, I am one blessed mama. I am forever grateful that despite seventeen pregnancies in total, more than half ended well, even when I had babies that ended up in special care.

Grief taught me a lot about myself. It taught me that it cracks you wide open and exposes you to people and things you wouldn't usually have experienced. It showed me the best and worst of people. It made me scared and vulnerable. I felt weak at times. I felt sad that my body couldn't just do what it was supposed to do, what it was designed for. I felt like a failure. I felt lost. And it's really hard for someone else to stand in the space of grief with you when they haven't endured what you have. It's really easy for someone else to say, "It wasn't meant to be!" or, "Don't worry, you'll have another baby!" But the what-ifs and the lack of understanding are the things that hurt the most.

Grief is indefinable. It is different for everyone. And if you've never been through it, you cannot truly understand it. Trying to describe it is a little like trying to tell someone what the bitterness of a lemon tastes like when they've never tasted one. "The Grief Club" is not a club you ever want to join—it's not a club you can ever leave. While, for me, time has dulled the sadness somewhat and I have ten beautiful children to enjoy, as well as one grandchild now, my seven Angels are never forgotten. I celebrate their lives on one specific day throughout the year, rather than seven different days, which would just drag out the sorrow. They each have a bauble with their names on for the Christmas tree, and I have framed plaques for each of them because naming them honoured them, and was an acknowledgment that they are part of my family, and always will be.

I think of them and I celebrate being their mama. I am grateful for each little Angel, who I hope to someday meet … knowing that greeting will be bittersweet, and thanking them for being part of my life, no matter how short our time together was.

Meekehleh Deserio

Meekehleh Deserio was born in Brisbane, Australia and worked as a freelance writer for over 30 years, in Australia, New York and LA, writing for many digital and hardcopy publications as well as working as Editor on several Blogs during her career in the Writing and Marketing arenas. Her love affair with writing began in primary school and her long literary journey was spurned from there. She now has ten book titles of her own, publishing under name of Lehlah Rio. Meekehleh is the mother of ten earth angels and seven in heaven. She has almost completed a law degree and looks forward to specialising in Human Rights Law.

The Moment Our Family Became Stronger

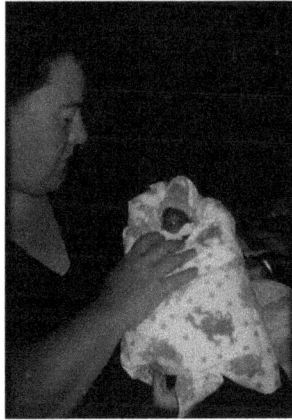

After having five healthy full-term pregnancies to my ex-husband, I was excited when I fell pregnant to my current partner. We had met just months before we found out and were both over the moon as he had two kids from a previous partner that he saw every second weekend.

It was February when I had the usual symptoms and took a pregnancy test to confirm it. I had some spotting but the doctor said all was good. Things were going great!

I had done something to my back so my doctor prescribed a strong painkiller (Panadeine forte), which I had never taken in other pregnancies. He said it was safe for the baby; I wasn't too sure but figured he knew what he was talking about.

I had one ultrasound at the X-ray clinic and, because I had accidentally double-booked, one at the local hospital ten days later. The first scan showed a healthy baby boy; everything was perfect. Then I went to the hospital scan, not thinking anything bad was going to happen.

The sonographer seemed to be looking for something. I've had enough scans to know what they are measuring and looking for, and I knew right then that something was wrong. I said to her, "There's no heartbeat, is there?" She said, "I just have to get my supervisor." A new person came in and put her hand on my arm and didn't say anything. I said, "There isn't any heartbeat, is there? So what do we do now?"

They asked me to come back on Monday—it was Friday— and they would do a repeat scan. We went home and broke it to all the kids and family that there was a chance I would be going to hospital on Monday and not coming home that night. The kids were devastated and so were we.

On Monday, I had my bag packed ready to go. We arrived at 8am, ready for the scan. It was confirmed that our baby boy had grown his Angel wings. So I went in to "mum mode," or robot mode. I said, "Okay, now what happens?" They sat us in a little room with three chairs and a little table with a box of tissues on it. My partner, Ben, looked at it and said to me, "This is weird," and I had to agree with him. Eventually the social worker came and spoke to us. She said we had to go to the delivery room and get things going.

They inserted a tablet to bring on the labour and they put us in the observation room as the other room they had was soundproof, had a TV, and a double bed—but a young girl was in there with her mum as she was losing twins.

We said, "It's okay, she needs the room more than us."

Ben and I tried distracting ourselves by what was in the room, such as why they kept certain items in the draws with other items (for example, vomit bags and straws together). Like the old saying goes, "If you don't laugh, you cry," so this kept us in good spirits when things started to happen.

I got a few niggles but nothing serious so I ate my dinner and Ben's dinner as well. I shouldn't have done that because the pains got worse so I called for the gas. There was no way I wanted to feel this if I didn't have my boy to keep. I ended up vomiting from the gas, first time ever that has happened to me!

At 9pm on 27 June 2011, our baby boy was born still inside the amniotic sack. I was twenty-two weeks pregnant and he was perfect. I got to hold him and the nurse asked Ben if we had any names yet. We didn't, but Ben chose to name him Robert Edward Buckley after his friends, and it was also a family name. Ben went home to the kids after a while but I kept Robert with me until the next day. We had decided not to let the kids see him as they were at that time aged between four and twelve years old. They got to see photos of him that the nurse took the next day, but he was starting to deteriorate by then as he had passed up to ten days earlier and had absorbed some of the fluid.

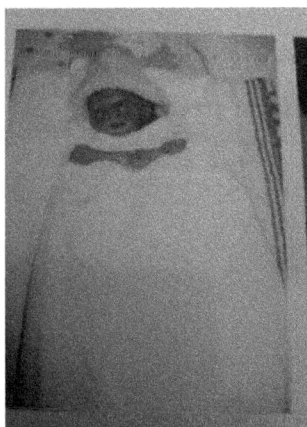

I said my goodbyes to Robert but still hadn't shed a tear. I had to be strong for the rest of the family. We came home and started planning the funeral; we decided on a cremation. It was a small event with a couple of family members there.

I still didn't cry.

Fast forward to November 2011, near to Robert's due date, and I started to feel sick. I thought it must have been thoughts of Robert, but I thought I'd take a few pregnancy tests anyway. They were all negative but I had all the familiar symptoms. I think altogether; I took six tests. On Robert's due date—4 November—I took another one. I was pregnant! We decided not to say anything until I was twelve weeks.

The pregnancy loss coordinator who helped us was amazing with the loss of Robert and rang me to let us know the autopsy results. There was no known cause of death. I joked around with Ben and said, "Your mum wanted him more than we did," as his mum had passed three years earlier. A couple of years later, I found out her actual time and date of passing. It was 9pm, on 27 June 2008, the same time and date as Robert's passing but three years earlier! I had instant goose bumps and said to Ben, "See, I told you!"

When I was twelve weeks pregnant with this new baby, we decided to tell everyone, which happened to fall on Christmas Day and the whole family was there which was good.

On 3 January 2012, I had a Down Syndrome screening ultrasound done at a private clinic. When we got there, we were excited. Then the nurse said, "I'm sorry, there is no heartbeat."

I said, "You have to be kidding me, right?"

I did everything right this time. I cried and cried. I cried for Robert, and I cried for Tad (that's the nickname we had for him as we didn't know what sex he was yet). I told Ben I was sorry but he said he was sorry. We both felt guilty and like failures.

We came home and told the kids and their response was,

"Not again!" This time, I had to see my GP on the way home and he told me to ring the early pregnancy loss clinic. They told me that I could wait and my body would miscarry but it could be up to six weeks, or they could book me in. I told them that I had delivered a stillborn six months earlier and if this baby had passed away, then I wanted it out of me NOW! So I had a D&C done. I asked them to do testing to see if Ben and I were compatible to have a child together and the reply was yes. We also found out Tad was a boy and we had lost him to Down Syndrome.

I want to help others get through what we have been through. I want to let others know that it does get better. Since losing my boys, I have completed a diploma in management and one in community services; I am also now a certified Birth and Bereavement Doula.

Ben is okay now but he didn't want to try and have another one. Losing the boys totally broke him and the kids had to go to grief counseling. My middle boy was showing aggression at school and saying things about death and dying which lead us to get the kids counseling; what came out in the counseling was that he felt it was his fault they died because he hugged me too tight. I explained that it wasn't, and he has come a long way since then. He still struggles with anger and is a very emotional teenager, but all the kids have coped really well with what they have been through. They miss their baby brothers, but it's brought us closer together as a family.

On the 24th November 2018, we will officially be a family as Ben and I get married. We will have been together for eight years on this day and we have been through so much. Earlier this year, Ben suffered a heart attack and had to have two stents put in, but he is doing a lot better. He has good days and bad, so I have put my Doula work on hold for now.

Dani Buckley

I'm Dani Buckley—I have five children, two step-children, two Angels, and live at Bribie Island, Queensland.

I am a volunteer in the community services sector working in emergency relief, and I also volunteer at the local Butterfly House, which I love. Additionally, I am involved with the local Maritime Safety Military Cadets as four of my children have either done or are doing cadets at this time.

I am a fully certified Birth and Bereavement Doula since going through our loss; below is our story.

Trials & Tribulations

At thirty-eight-years-old, this is my fifth and final pregnancy. I have one living child. My husband and I long for another baby, a sibling for our son. But at our age and with our history, our financial and emotional resources are depleted. We need to start thinking about saving for retirement, and those funds have been depleted in our efforts to have a family.

I am seven weeks along and lying on the table as the ultrasound technician searches around for a heartbeat. It is all too familiar to me, the silence except for the typing as she clicks here and there and measures this and that. She says the pregnancy is too small to see transabdominally (the ultrasound probe on the tummy with the gel that you see in all the movies). So, I will need to go empty my bladder. I just drank a ton of water, and I've been suffering for the past hour, needing to pee. So I follow the routine; I am always too small at this stage to see the baby from the outside. I go to the bathroom and return for the transvaginal. I'll spare you the details of that.

More silence, more clicking. More seconds ticking by. I've known I am pregnant for three weeks now and it all comes down to this second. Is there a heartbeat or not?

I didn't see my first pregnancy on ultrasound. I miscarried very early in my first trimester. It was as if my monthly cycle was just a few weeks late and I had a heavy period. Less than twenty percent of pregnancies end in miscarriage. But when you think about it, that is a lot of pregnancies ending early. After a heartbeat is detected, that risk falls to three percent.

There wasn't much concern at this point about me not being able to have a healthy baby. You know, many women experience early miscarriage. The body is very smart that way. If there is something wrong with the development of the baby, the body knows. The stars need to align. It is quite a miracle to get past the first trimester. That is why most people wait to announce their pregnancy until they are "safe." I didn't know it at the time, but I did eventually find out that there is no "safe zone" for me.

The second pregnancy, I was further along in my first trimester. I was spotting and didn't feel the typical early pregnancy symptoms. So I went in for an early ultrasound, and there was no heartbeat. I remember the doctor being called in and he said he was sorry. He wanted to get another doctor to look and confirm his findings. The other doctor took a look and said how very sorry he was. I was sad about the loss. I was starting to become worried that I could not carry a baby to term. The doctor advised me that they don't really investigate further until there are three early losses.

A couple of years later, I hadn't conceived again. Now it was time to investigate the dreaded infertility problem. I had a tubal dye study done to make sure my tubes weren't blocked. Turns out, the dye wasn't getting through one of the tubes. But I still had the other one. I had an exploratory procedure done called a laparoscopy. They go in with a camera through two small incisions in my abdomen to look around at my reproductive system. Other than some scar tissue, which they cleared, everything looked good in and around my uterus. The doctor put me on a drug called Clomid. It didn't work. I didn't want to go down the road further into the infertility treatments. My husband and I decided to see what the future held and not worry about it. We believe in God, and we believed that we would have children if it was meant to be.

Fast forward almost eight years. We hadn't been actively trying or worried about having a baby. Just as I had prepared myself for the real possibility that we may be a childless couple, I got a BFP. That is pregnancy talk for "big fat positive."

I spotted early on with my third pregnancy, and I had several ultrasounds. At around fourteen weeks, I was standing with my workgroup and felt a gush of blood. Luckily, I was wearing a pad and saved myself some huge embarrassment. An ultrasound revealed that the baby was developing splendidly, and there was no explanation for the bleed. Some women just bleed throughout pregnancy, they said. My twenty-week ultrasound was normal. We did not want to find out the gender. We were looking for a surprise. Boy, did we get one, but not in the way we were expecting.

At twenty-four weeks, I started spotting. I had a sensation that the baby was kicking straight down. I joked with my sister, "He can't break out of here, can he?" I went to the emergency room on Saturday night at exactly twenty-four weeks. They listened to the heartbeat and sent me home. They said to follow up with my doctor on Monday. The spotting stopped and I felt fine by Monday. The nurse called and left me a message. She heard that I had been in the ER, and if I felt that they should take a look, I could come in for an ultrasound. I felt silly at this point. I mean, I had been spotting my entire pregnancy. There was a heartbeat. I felt like I was being an over-worried pain in the butt to my doctor. I did not go in, a decision I came to regret.

Exactly one week later, on Saturday night, my husband and I went to bed at midnight. We had been up late preparing the nursery for our little one. We went to the craft store and painted little animal plaques for the wall. We painted the room and set up the furniture. It was quite an accomplishment. I was feeling extremely sore and tired but assumed it was from all the painting. I had to go to the bathroom, but every time I tried, nothing would come out. Finally, I fell asleep. Two hours later, at 2am, I got up again to go to the bathroom. I felt a gush and my waters broke all over my bathroom floor.

My son was born that night, by emergency C-section, at exactly twenty-five weeks gestation. He weighed one pound, eleven and a half ounces, and was twelve inches long. Having a twenty-five-week micro-preemie is a story in and of itself. In summary, we spent one hundred and four days in the NICU (Neonatal Intensive Care Unit), including an ambulance transport to and from a major metropolitan area for heart surgery involving complications. Due to his extremely underdeveloped lungs, he was on home oxygen for the first few years of his life. We gave him nebuliser treatments frequently. It is fair to say that we have been sleep deprived for the past four and a half years.

When my son was almost two years old, he became critically ill with a respiratory infection. He was airlifted to Children's Hospital in Minneapolis, where he spent six weeks on a ventilator. His lungs were unable to oxygenate his blood so he had to go on a lung bypass machine called ECMO. He was on ECMO only four days when he began bleeding out and was rushed into emergency surgery to repair an ulcer.

My son has been within seconds of death so many times in his short life. I believed in God before my son was born, but if I had any doubt in the existence of miracles, that is completely gone now. I know for a fact that Jesus held my boy in His healing hands and gave him comfort and healing during his ordeal. I felt Him. I know beyond a reasonable doubt that my son is here today due to divine intervention. Finding faith through trauma is another fascinating subject for another story and another time. But this story is not done. Our trauma did not end here.

When my son was three years old, fully recovered from his critical illness and rehabilitated (he had to learn to eat and walk and everything all over again), I found out I was pregnant for the fourth time. We were ecstatic that we were going to have another child. I went to a high-risk OBGYN this time and was being monitored closely.

One of the ultrasounds showed a growth very near my cervix that was suspected to be a uterine polyp. I was referred to a perinatologist for a stitch (cerclage). The polyp was not reachable for removal and it was decided not to place a cerclage. There was a risk of hitting the polyp and causing hemorrhaging. Since my cervix was long and closed, the recommendation was to keep monitoring me closely. I started Makena, a hormone shot, at sixteen weeks. Progesterone is the hormone in this shot, and it helps the body stay pregnant.

At seventeen and a half weeks, my waters broke. I was placed on complete bed rest. The prognosis was not good, but there was still a chance I could make it to twenty-three weeks, at which time I would be placed on hospital bed rest and attempts would be made to save the baby. I had no fluid left. At my nineteen and a half week appointment, my baby had no heartbeat. I was induced and gave natural birth to my Angel, Isaac David. He is buried in my husband's family cemetery.

We spent a lot of time grieving Isaac's death and then trying to figure out if we would ever try again. We wanted another child. We wanted our son to have a sibling. We definitely did not want to put another child through the NICU experience. We did not want to experience any more loss. Financially, we were spent. We were back in the thought pattern that we would not be having any more children. A year and a half after Isaac, we decided we were going to try one more time. We would give it three cycles. If it was meant to be, it was meant to be. If not, we were content to know that our son was an only child and another baby was not in the plan for us. We got pregnant on the first try.

I cannot describe to you the nervous and sad emotions that come with pregnancy after a loss. On that ultrasound table at seven weeks, my fifth pregnancy revealed a heartbeat. There is a little life growing inside me as I type this story. I don't know how the story will end. I am not optimistic. I am not feeling joy. I was happy to see a heartbeat, but I don't want to share the news with anybody until I make it to twenty-four weeks. In the US, twenty-four weeks (and sometimes twenty-two and twenty-three weeks) is the point that the doctors are willing to take measures to save babies.

Until then, I am just waiting. Waiting to see if this baby makes it. Waiting to see blood at any time. Waiting to feel movement. Waiting until the next ultrasound to see if there is progress. Every pain, every twinge, makes me worried that I am losing this baby. Just waiting and praying for a happy ending.

But like I said earlier, there is no "safe zone" for me. I will either have a living, crying baby in my arms or I won't. It isn't up to me to decide.

On 18 April 2016, we welcomed a healthy little girl into our family. She was born at thirty-seven weeks and weighed six pounds, ten and a half ounces. She was seventeen point seventy-five inches long. We are relieved after a very stressful pregnancy to have our family, now complete.

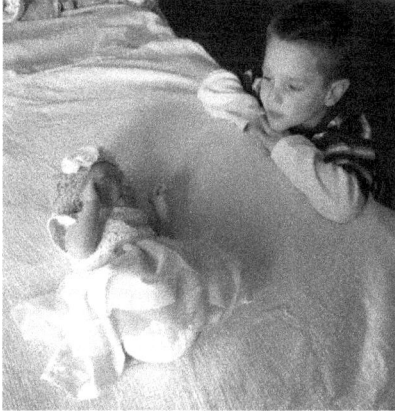

Photographs by Beautiful Lens Photography

Jenny Tiernan St. Cloud, Minnesota, USA

Twins Forever

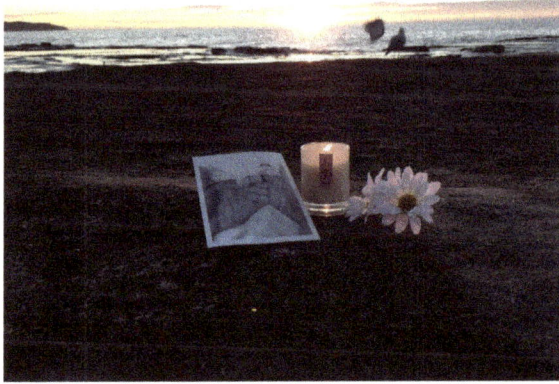

Dear Sophie and Jasmine,

This is the story of your journey together as identical twins and the challenges we faced throughout our pregnancy, and our experience with Twin to Twin Transfusion Syndrome and how this changed our world as we once saw it more than we would have ever been able to imagine.

The Day We Found Out About You
October 30th 2015

I took a pregnancy test, and to my surprise, it was positive. I was so nervous; I didn't know what to do. I couldn't wait for Tyson (Daddy) to get home from work! I rushed to the doctors to confirm it was real and on my way home, I bought a card to tell him the exciting news.

He had gotten home early from work and was wondering where I was, and as I walked through the door, I couldn't look him in the eyes without bursting out into tears of joy. I handed him the card I had signed quickly outside the supermarket, but he wouldn't open it.

He kept saying, "What's going on? Why are you being weird? What's wrong with you?"

He finally opened it … his eyes filled with tears and he had a huge smile on his face. We were both overjoyed; we were going to have a baby!

Our First Scan
November 18th 2015 – Week Six

We decided to have an early dating scan as we didn't know the date of conception. We were waiting in anticipation for the first time we would get to meet you (even if on a screen). There you were, just a single dot inside my tummy, looking at us from the other side of the screen.

Then, Daddy spotted something on the other side of the sac, another little spot. He didn't say anything to me; I think he was in shock!

The nurses were chatting away and started giggling and said, "Is that two I can see?"

I suddenly realised what was going on and it was announced that we were having twins! Daddy and I looked at each other, and we both cried and laughed; we were over the moon. We were also in shock. Twins! We were so excited and couldn't wait to tell all our family.

We started planning all the fun ways to tell your grandparents and aunties and uncles.

Our Week Ten Scan
December 10th 2015 – Week Ten

We decided to have a scan called the NIPT Test to screen for any abnormalities and also to determine if you were going to be boys or girls.

We had so much joy seeing you at our scans, just chilling out enjoying your early days together. Our nurse could now tell that you were both in one egg, separated by a tiny membrane (sac), which meant you were going to be IDENTICAL TWINS!

Our excitement continued to grow.

The Big First Trimester Scan
December 30th 2015 – Week Thirteen

We had now been pregnant with you for over three months, and the scan went really well. You both looked healthy and were growing well and we were out of the first trimester. This meant we could share our news with the world. What an exciting way to start 2016!

A couple of weeks later, we received a phone call from our nurse with the results from our NIPT Test. All our tests came back clear, such wonderful news. We also were told that they were unable to find any Y chromosomes, and they could only find the X …this meant we were having GIRLS, identical twin girls!!!!!

Daddy was of course hoping for boys, but that didn't last long and he soon was over the moon with the thought of having daughters. He started to imagine all those boys turning up to take you girls on dates and how he'd be waiting with the shotgun.

The Start of Our TTTS Journey
Week commencing January 18th, 2016 – Week Sixteen Scan

It is routine for mothers expecting twins to have a scan at sixteen weeks. This was the day we found out about Twin to Twin Transfusion Syndrome, something we had never heard about. We were showing early signs of TTTS and were told we would need a follow-up scan in a week at the Royal North Shore Hospital in St. Leonards.

This was a very scary week researching TTTS, as it's a very scary disease with little information available online. We decided to wait and talk to the doctors the following week. We knew we had to stay strong for you.

It was so lovely to see both of you moving around at each scan. By sixteen weeks, you were both so big and strong and you loved to kick and play with each other. It brought us so much joy watching you play together.

Reality Hit Us Hard
Week Seventeen

TTTS can affect twins who share a placenta (monochromic twins) and occurs when there is an imbalance in the placental blood vessels that connect the twins. One twin gets too much blood (called the recipient twin) and the other too little (called the donor twin). This results in the recipient twin producing extra fluid which can put a strain on the heart, and the donor twin will have little or none, meaning slow growth.

There are five stages of TTTS, and each pregnancy can vary the stage it reaches. Some mothers can remain at stage one and continue a healthy pregnancy and sadly, other progress to stage five which is where one of both of the twins pass away from severe TTTS.

During our follow-up scan at the Royal North Shore Hospital, we were informed we had progressed to stage one TTTS. We could not believe our luck and could not believe that we had this disease. The doctors told us that they are yet to understand why some mothers with identical twins get TTTS and others do not.

Why us? we asked ourselves. Why us?

Our doctor advised us that we would be referred to the Royal Hospital for Women in Randwick to visit the TTTS expert on further recommendations on the best plan of action to help save you both, our beautiful babies.

Our Options
February 1st 2016 - Week Eighteen

At this appointment, our scan showed that we had progressed to stage two TTTS. Twin One was not showing a bladder, which meant you girls could soon be in a critical condition.

We were then given all the many difficult options:
1. To terminate our babies
2. To undergo fetal laser surgery
3. To wait out and hope that it went away (this was unlikely for cases that had progressed to stage two so quickly)

We didn't even need to discuss this and we both knew we wanted to try the surgery. This was the only option to save you baby girls.

The SURGERY
February 2nd 2016 – Week Eighteen

This was a very long day for us all. Daddy had to work so Aunty Miki (my sister) came to be with me. The procedure was relatively quick and I was very high on drugs to stop the pain. At the end of the surgery, the doctors asked me if I wanted to see what they had done. I looked up on to the screen and could see inside my tummy. It was like watching a scene from a David Attenborough show in HD.

And right then, I saw you for the first time; I saw your little foot moving around. It was a beautiful image I will never forget.

The next twenty-four hours were one of the hardest of my life, waiting to see if you both were still alive. I was wheelchaired into the scan room and they placed the ultrasound on my tummy … there you both were, both moving, two little heartbeats pumping away.

I cried and cried with joy, and at the moment, I felt like the proudest mum, knowing I had two strong little fighters.

The Wait

For the next week, we waited, as this is still a risky period. But a week later, we had a scan and all looked well; the surgery had worked. Both of you were doing wonderfully. The fluid levels had evened out and we were back on our way, and I finally hoped for some time to relax.

Week Twenty Scan
February 19th 2016

The doctors took a while during this scan, looking at all the different parts of you both to make sure all your blood flows were going well. However, they noticed that the blood flow to our donor baby, Twin One's brain was showing signs of Twin Anemia Polycythemia Sequence (TAPS).

TAPS is another condition in twins where the blood flow is unequal but different from TTTS. The unequal blood counts can mean that one twin will not receive the nutrients and oxygen it needs to develop properly due to an imbalance of red blood cells and haemoglobin. TAPS can occur randomly in silo or after an incomplete foetal laser surgery to treat TTTS.

The worry, the fear; it all started all over again. We were not out of the woods yet.

So-Called "Conservative Management"
Weeks Twenty-One – Twenty-Six

We were told by our doctor that there was nothing more that we could do apart from "wait and see and hope for the best." This is the last thing you want to be told by the one person you trust the most.

Every week we came in for our scan, not knowing if you babies would be alive. Our doctor advised that we did not qualify for surgery again because the first time was difficult enough and it was a bigger risk to the babies, and we were too early to deliver.

I did some of my own research and found some successful stories in the past where mothers drank protein shakes and went on bedrest. So I started to try that; I drank protein drinks every day and rested when I could.

Each week, we monitored the TAPS, which resulted in our donor twin developing anaemia (Twin One) and our recipient developing polycythemia (Twin Two); the results were slowly improving week by week, you both were getting stronger and so were we. Your strength gave us strength.

We loved seeing you every week, and my heart stopped beating just before each scan until I would see you on the screen and could see you moving and your hearts beating. Every week you kept on fighting. You played together and grew together, keeping each other strong. That was where your lives started, together inside my womb.

As I had an anterior placenta, I was unable to feel your kicks, so seeing so much movement in the scans each week was reassuring.

At twenty-six weeks, I went for the routine gestational diabetes check-up, and not surprisingly I had GD. It's quite common to get it with twins, so nothing alarming there. I just had to watch my diet and check my sugar levels a few times a day. It was stressful, but I got into a routine.

Unexpected Symptoms
Week Twenty-Seven and Twenty-Eight

At week twenty-seven, you were both looking great, the TAPS had gone, and you were both back to being normal. We couldn't believe it, we were in the clear and could once again relax and try to enjoy the last trimester.

Because of the GD and the improvements with you, our doctor decided to move our scan forward for convenience to the Tuesday; we were originally due on the following Friday. As all looked great on the scan on Tuesday, our doctor said we could push back to two weeks before coming back. I was nervous and didn't think it was right, but he was adamant and you always trust your doctor.

However, that Friday night (the day of the original scan) at twenty-eight-weeks and one day, I started getting severe upper abdominal pain and mild contractions, which we thought may have been Braxton Hicks. I went into emergency and waited five hours; the doctors checked you babies with a heart monitor only and sent me home.

As the week went on, I grew more nervous day by day. I had lots of stomach tightening, happening every ten minutes, and occasional upper abdominal pains. I tried to get an earlier scan, but my doctor was unavailable. I was also growing rapidly and my stomach was solid.

The Final Scan
Week Twenty-Nine

On Friday, at twenty-nine weeks and one day, I had my scan, and to no surprise, I was showing signs of TTTS again. The fluid discordance was nine centimeters in the recipient and three centimeters in the donor.

The doctor told me it was okay, that it was just signs and I'd be okay over the weekend, and to chill out and stop worrying. He booked me in for a scan on the following Tuesday (as the Monday was a public holiday), and advised that I should come prepared to deliver in case I worsened over the weekend.

On Saturday, I'd had enough. I *knew* something was wrong. I went into emergency again waited another five hours and the nurses monitored your heart beats. It took them so long to find the heartbeats of both of you.

Even then, you don't know if it's different babies. I pushed them to call my obstetrician. They said they couldn't on a weekend, but I pushed them to get an ultrasound and they did that at least. The doctor on-call came and looked at the ultrasound and said, "Both heartbeats are fine, stop worrying."

I noticed on the ultrasound that one of your bladders looked huge. I couldn't see the other's bladder. I pointed this out to the doctor and the nurse, and the doctor turned the scan machine away from me and said, "All is fine."

I was even told by the nurse later on to "stop Googling." I was unfortunately seen by inexperienced, negligent medical staff that did not know about TTTS and did not know what they should have been looking for on that scan. They were short and quick to get me out.
I was considered one of the most high-risk pregnancies that hospital had come through the doors and I was pushed out the door and told to come back on Tuesday.

I knew something was wrong; a mother's instinct is always right. I even had my bags packed the day I went to emergency. The medical system let me down. I trusted them when I should have gone with my gut.

The Day You Cuddled Your Sister Goodbye
Twenty-Nine Weeks and Six Days

On Tuesday, I went in for my scan. That moment I had feared for the past eight weeks became a reality. I vaguely remember hearing the words, "We have lost a heartbeat," then the nurse running out to get the obstetrician. He came in; he looked ... it was real, no heartbeat in our donor baby.

Everything stopped for a moment life stopped, our world was about to change so much more than we would have ever been able to imagine. I thought my heart was going to stop too, but then it hit me; my other baby, is she okay, is she beating? And you were, you were still fighting.

You had to say goodbye to your sister who passed away right next to you. What a star. I knew there was no chance we were going to lose you too. I was making the decisions from now; I had lost all faith in the hospital at that point.

They gave us two options: one, to deliver Twin Two the next day, or to try and wait out a few more weeks. There was abnormal blood flow in Twin Two, and there was no way I was leaving you in there. You were ready, and we were ready to meet you.

The Delivery
That night, as I went to sleep, I made a wish…

I wish that you, my beautiful baby girl, stay strong and make it through until tomorrow. I promise I will give you the best life I can and be the best mother I know how to be, and that we will always keep the memory of your sister Sophie alive.

The next day on Wednesday, April 27th we delivered both you girls by emergency caesarean. Donor baby Twin One, we named Sophie Louise. She was born first, sleeping at 9:11am and weighed eight hundred and fifty grams. She was brought straight to our side. There were no cries, just silence.

Recipient baby Twin Two ... we later named you Jasmine Nicholai Sophie. You were born second at 9:12am, and you weighed one point two pounds, and the sound of your cries gave us so much joy during that bittersweet moment. You were rushed off to the NICU immediately; Daddy stayed by my side, and we kept Sophie close to us that morning.

Your Days in the NICU

You spent the next eight weeks in the Neonatel Intensive Care Unit (NICU) where you were so strong. We could not have been more proud! Each week you grew a little stronger and a little bit bigger.

Jasmine, you are our miracle and the most important little being in our world.

Meeting Your Sister Sophie

We are so sorry you didn't get to meet your beautiful sister
Sophie. But I know you had so much fun with her in my
tummy.
Sophie will always be with you, and she will be in our hearts
forever.
We are so lucky to have had you both, our beautiful twins.
Sophie was born sleeping; we had a couple of days to cuddle
her and have her by our side.

Jessica Burdus

Jessica Burdus lives in Sydney with her fiance, 3 children,
two beautiful identical twins, one in her arms and one in
her heart, and a rainbow baby boy. 2 years ago Jessica and
her family experienced the deadly condition Twin to Twin
Transfusion Syndrome with their first pregnancy resulting
in the loss of one twin. This experience has changed Jessica's
outlook on life more that she could have imagined. Jessica is
a volunteer with the TTTS Australia Incorporated Company.
Jessica's aim with her story is to help support families dealing
with baby loss and spread awareness of this terrible condition. As no twins should ever walk alone.

To the Newly Bereaved Parent

Please Know that You're Not Alone

This was extremely hard to write and share; in a world full of supportive people, we have certainly felt alone because it's such a taboo and people are scared to talk about anything to do with the loss of a child. Unfortunately, we live in a world where we as humans are judged for what shoes we wear, what house we live in, and whether we like boys or girls, so when we had to make a heartbreaking choice, we became fearful of what people would think.

The reality is that you are not in our shoes and you never will be. Even if you have to take the same path as us, your story will still be different. Although we wish this would never happen to anyone, the reality is once you get outside the bubble you live in; it's everywhere. Many people are silently grieving, too afraid to let people know what is going on because they are scared of judgement. I've met some of the strongest mothers and heard their stories, some full term, miscarriages, and terminations, and the way other people treat their child as if they don't exist weeks after they've gone through the toughest struggle is appalling. It took me almost twelve months to grieve my best friend passing away; she was my puppy of fifteen years.

"Getting over" a child passing away will not happen in weeks, months, or years because you don't get over them. They are a part of you forever. I feel if we share her story and someone you know or perhaps years down the track your children or children's children have to face something like this, you might be able to say that you knew people who went through this and you know that they survived and made it through.

This story is about our daughter, Chloe. I should have a baby in my arms today. And instead, we are trying to find our "new normal." This story is about a time of survival, learning how strong your marriage is, courage, loyalty, friendships, love, and a shitty, unfair situation.

I'm not writing it so you will feel sorry for us—we have done enough of that for ourselves—but more for awareness and to #breakthesilence. It's to help us in our grieving process because bumping into people in the street that don't know our story is terrifying.

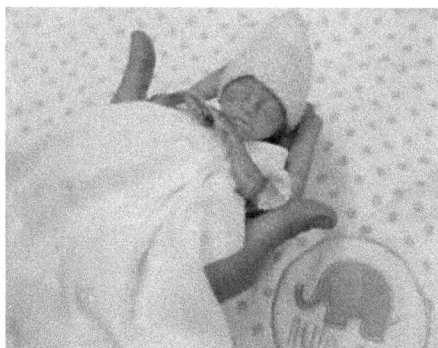

On the 30th of April 2016, we should have been welcoming a precious bundle of joy into our lives; listening to her cry, changing her nappy, watching her smile and grow and instead, we will release balloons and blow out candles on a cake on behalf of her. We were faced with a decision that we would never wish upon anyone. We planned a funeral when others listened to their baby's beautiful cry. We set a baby room up for our little girl and this room remains empty.

She was sent to be with the angels at only twenty-one weeks gestation.

Her name is Chloe Fay Mason. She is the daughter of Troy and Zena Mason and although you can't physically see her in our arms, she existed. She was twenty-six centimeters. She had my nose and the rest of her was her daddy. She had long feet and hands, little specs of blonde hair, and she was ours. Made with love! And certainly missed.

On the 10th of December, we went for our twenty-week scan, right on Troy's birthday. What a cool present this would be to find out if our baby was to be a girl or a boy, right? We were in the safe zone. We thought that nothing could go wrong.

The ultrasound technician couldn't tell us the sex, though he did mention that the baby yawned and waved at us. He failed to mention why he was paying particular attention to her spine and brain. Mostly, he was silent the whole way through. Little did we know that this was the start of something much bigger.

We were surprised when we were called into the hospital on the 14th December. This is where we were told that we were having a baby girl and then hit with information that our little Chloe was not well. She had Spina Bifida, hydrocephalus, and Arnold Chiari malformation.

What this basically meant was that she had a lot of spinal fluid on her brain, she had a lemon-shaped head, and they could see issues with her spine and an open pocket on her back exposing her spinal cord. This pocket normally closes off during the first few weeks after conception.

We were told if she were to survive, to even make it to full term, she would be straight into the operating theatre at not even a day old to have a permanent stent put into her brain to drain the fluid build-up that she would forever have.

She would then go into an operation to close the opening on her spine to stop her exposed spinal cords from showing and getting infected. This wouldn't fix the problem as the damage already happened when she was two to four weeks gestation. Although some parents might live with this, their story is not ours, and we're all not the same.

We walked into that room wanting to find out the sex of the baby and walked out with a heavy heart and what felt like a house sitting on our shoulders. The doctor told us the outlook on her life would be grim. She would be brain dead, she wouldn't be able to walk, we would be changing nappies for the rest of her life and she would be in a wheelchair.

The doctor gave us two choices; to end the pregnancy or to continue it, knowing that if Chloe made it full term, we would have support. I used to think the hardest decision I would have with a child was what school they would go to or whether or not to breastfeed. But choosing whether your child should live or die is by far the hardest.

We waited for the doctor to write up all this information in a room full of happily expecting pregnant ladies but we were distraught, our brains were going one million miles an hour, and we still had to drive home.

When we got home, we were silent; we had no idea what to do. Googling what we had heard had never seemed so important and somehow, Troy and I had to come together in the end to be on the same page. I searched Spina Bifida pages, and I found all the fabulous stories of the children who have parts of Chloe's diagnosis but what I had to realise is every story is different.

Zena and Troy Mason said goodbye to the baby daughter in a small ceremony and scattered some of her ashes in the ocean.

After many consultations with doctors and lots of tears, we chose to take the pain now, so our Chloe didn't have to. We didn't want to bring a child into the world just to have her exist without living. Would she even know that we existed? What life would she have? The guilt we live with every day would never be as painful as it would be to watch as she grew without growing.

A board of doctors had to approve our decision and when they did, I was admitted to the hospital.

I was induced and gave birth to Chloe on the morning of the 19th December (right in between Troy's and my birthday) with limited pain relief—I felt I needed to take some pain for our little girl. And I will tell you now, the labour stories people gave me when I was pregnant will never scare me because nothing can quite prepare you for the birth of your baby, let alone to a little angel.

When little Chloe was put into our arms, we couldn't celebrate because this is what ended her life. She didn't cry; she didn't move; she was cold and we were numb.

We spent a full day with her, dressed her, gave her kisses

because she was our beautiful girl and this would be the last time we would ever see her and those moments would have to last a lifetime.

She had the obvious signs of her diagnosis, a lemon-shaped malformed skull and the Spina Bifida sacral lesion on her back.

We can't get any of those moments back, but we were lucky enough to get precious photos of her from Heartfelt Photography so we can never forget her face.

She had family and friends visit her as well as flowers and cards from beautiful people across the state. Chloe got cuddles from her aunties and uncles and grandma.

Every day after, we woke up, and we wished it was all a big nightmare. I would look down at my tummy and see a belly that was empty. I only recognised her movements after she was no longer in me. If going through labour wasn't enough, your hormones are so messed up and to make matters worse, the breast decides it might pay a visit.

Life sucked completely for the first month after she was born. Even though you have just had a baby, people fail to realise that you should be taking it easy because there is no physical sign of a child. Conversations are awkward because no one knows what to say and everyone looks at you with sad eyes. The simplest of tasks are a big effort and some days I felt like I was a two-year-old chucking a tantrum.

I couldn't have got through without my amazing husband.

Chloe was in getting her autopsy done, and this would take three weeks. On my birthday, we were asked if they could keep her brain and spine as they were running behind. We told them to take their time in hope it might shed some more light.

We never imagined our pregnancy to end this way; after all, no one shares the terrible stories. Each week was something new. First we had to find items to have with her for the cremation, visiting her in her itty bitty coffin with all the special tokens that grandmas and aunts had provided (photos of her cousins, letters, and drawings), her birth certificate arriving, her ashes, her death certificate, cards in the mail, donations and preparation for her ceremony.

When would getting all these triggers end?

It was then time we had to go back to the hospital. We talked to the doctor about everything that had happened. We were advised the chance of this happening again would be very unlikely. We asked, "Why did this happen?" I took my prenatal vitamins before Chloe was conceived. We ate well. I lost twenty kilograms, I didn't drink, and my husband quit smoking.

We had a ceremony for Chloe on Australia Day at the place where we got married. We had a balloon to release, but Chloe decided it would be better to go earlier and it was released in the car. Chloe had around thirty people come (more would have) and we had a lovely celebrant say some beautiful things. We had some tables set up with some of her special items, her birth certificate, her pictures, teddies, funeral books, and memory jars made just for her. We then spread a small amount of ashes in the ocean and blew bubbles. It was perfect and heart-warming that we had so much support from our amazing friends and family.

The situation we have been in has been very awful, but my husband and I are stronger than ever. We have learnt a lot about true friends and family, and the support we have received from the Facebook world has been nothing short of amazing, even when I'm having tantrums. The messages, the calls, the cards, the flowers, the thoughts, and the kind words.

The support from our work, the assistance from the hospital and the doctors, it makes us feel so lucky and appreciative in a time when luck was not on our side.

Sands—the support group for those affected by miscarriage, stillbirth and newborn death—was a great help. I was given a care pack in the hospital which contained some useful information from Sands. I read about so many other people who had gone through similar situations on the Sands website, but one particular story stood out. This story was that of a lady called Ali. Ali's experience was so close to what I went through. That night, I felt less alone and thought if she could survive, so could I. Since then, I have used Sands email support and have called the helpline on numerous occasions. Having the person at the other end really understand was so refreshing, especially in my times of need.

We personally wouldn't be where we are today without some key people in my life, new and old, virtual and real. I've met some people from all around the world on support groups for people in this terrible club. In a time when you feel so alone, you start to realise that you are not. To help my healing, I donated my wedding dress to Angel Gowns to make little angel dresses. I edited photos of other angels and put them into special wall features for their parents.

I've seen so much pain on these groups and if I could have any superpower, it would be to give everyone their babies back and let them have them forever.

When I hear people in the normal world complaining about something to do with their child, it does make me sad. This is because little things like being up late at night to crying, or teething, or fevers is a luxury in my new world. These things are things that mothers in this group would die to have. Hug your children and loved ones tightly and please enjoy these precious moments.

All kinds of tragedies strike when we least expect it and life shouldn't be taken for granted.

My husband went back to work in the new year and I was back at work on the 15th Feb which was nine weeks after her birth. Australia is amazing for recognising her birth and allowing me access maternity leave; however had she been nineteen weeks instead of twenty, we wouldn't have been so lucky which makes me sad. I've had the privilege of seeing many beautiful angels at all gestations, and I can tell you a baby is a baby as soon as it's conceived.

The emotional turmoil that is left whether for miscarriage, stillbirth, being in NICU, or terminating a pregnancy is huge, but to be told that they don't exist prior to twenty weeks is just awful. What hurts more is when people use words that make these big events in our lives less significant; think about what you say to people before you say it.

I used to be a big positive person! You would hear me say everything happens for a reason, but how can I say that now? Someone in the universe chose to give Chloe a terrible diagnosis, made us go through labour, death, and organising a funeral so I can learn?? I'd rather not have the lesson, thanks ... what child would you give up to learn a lesson in life?

If you're still reading, thank you! Chloe's story will only close when we allow it to and we won't. She will always be our first baby girl ... our child! Just because she isn't here doesn't mean she doesn't exist. She will be remembered until the day we die.

We waited ten years to make a perfect life for her; little did we know that nothing on the outside could have helped what was going on inside. We have no regrets with our decision; the only regret we have is not spending time with her in my tummy and worrying about others too much.

This year, we are being selfish in some instances and not feeling guilty for it. "Fit our oxygen masks first before helping others."

We ended a very much wanted pregnancy.

We have changed, parts of us are broken, but we're survivors, and we've survived so far.

Zena Mason

Hi, my name is Zena. I'm an admin officer, a wife, and a mother to two beautiful babies and a little girl called Chloe who is in the heavens and a rainbow toddler!

Rainbow After the Storm

When you hold your first born in your arms, time stands still You exist in a love bubble. You're overwhelmed with emotion at the thought of this precious child making you a mother. Making you parents.

"I'm a mother," went through my head many times as I gave birth to my son.

I couldn't wait to see him, hold him, and see who he looked like. I took in every part of my beautiful little bundle. Ten fingers, ten tiny toes, little button nose, his smell, the curve of his lips, the softness of his skin and downy hair. I will never forget that moment with my first born, my little Charlie Jacob.

Perfect and small. My hands, his daddy's lips, dark hair, a sweet smell, his beauty. Perfect in every way. These memories will last a lifetime and be etched in my mind forever. My lasting memory of a little boy I would never take home.

Charlie Jacob was born at nineteen weeks and one day,

weighing just two hundred and fifty-six grams. He was born breathing and lived for thirty minutes before he grew his angel wings.

A preterm loss due to "cervical incompetence."

I will never forget that day. It was the hottest day in sixty years: 8 January 2013.

I was experiencing pain the day prior but had no idea I was in labour. I thought it might be Braxton Hicks or stretching pains. Being in labour wasn't on my radar. I became concerned, so made my way to the hospital. I was examined and told I was three centimeters dilated, and sadly, that I was in labour and would be delivering my son with no chance of survival.

My world came crashing down.

Why us? Why this baby, the one we longed for and tried for, for seven years—with numerous IVF treatments, surgery investigations, countless tests, two early miscarriages, failed cycles, and cancelled cycles—to conceive. It didn't seem real. It was so unfair.

My IVF journey was an emotional rollercoaster I thought was over once I had finally conceived Charlie. He was our last embryo. I was relieved of the challenge of emotions I experienced for so long; the heartbreak and disappointment seemed to be over once I heard a healthy heartbeat at our eight-week scan.

Charlie arrived late in the afternoon on that day. He was perfect. I was in awe of how beautiful he was. He was perfectly formed, just incredibly small.

We had some time with him and then farewelled our little boy. We handed him to our midwife Nicolle, who I will never forget. She was so supportive. I will always be grateful to her. I saw her tears and heartbreak too.

Those brief moments with Charlie were wrenching, but special too, as with any birth; a moment in time etched in your mind forever.

I sat in the garden at the hospital the night that Charlie was born in a state of disbelief. I placed my hands on my belly, realising my hopes and dreams for him were gone. He was so wanted and he was gone. I was devastated but also incredibly proud. I felt very blessed despite the circumstances. I had become a mother that day to a precious little boy.

He's not here, but I'm still his mother and he's my son. My first born; my precious Angel.

The weeks that followed his loss were incredibly hard. Having to make arrangements for his final resting place, his cremation, our personal memorial service—all so hard and heartbreaking. A place we can visit and special songs are all that is left to remember him. Our song for him. "Somewhere over the Rainbow." A plaque etched with his name, and personal quote marks his resting place. Sentimental items have been placed lovingly with him. A position on the baby lawn that has the sun setting before him each day, near a set of stairs I would sit when visiting.

The love I held for Charlie helped me put one foot in front of the other in a personal journey that helped me learn so much about myself and what was really important. His loss made me reevaluate life as I knew it and made necessary steps for my recovery.

The grief that would come over me in waves was my new normal. Life fit in around it.

I walked with a different beat. I stopped rushing around and took time in everything I did. I used my senses to take in the beauty of my surroundings—smell the roses, so to speak, feel the warmth of the sun on my skin and a breeze blowing my hair. I slowed right down and took better care of myself. I had always put everyone ahead of myself, but now it was important to take a bit of that selflessness for myself. More self-care. Less work hours. I started saying no instead of yes all the time. I disconnected from those that bought negativity to my life. I wanted to feel free of chaos.

We decided to give IVF another go a short few months after losing Charlie. Walking back into the clinic was difficult. I never saw myself going back, except to show off the pride and joy they helped us bring into the world.

We were met with open arms and supported through the next chapter of our IVF journey. We were incredibly blessed to fall pregnant with a fresh transfer following egg collection. I was so relieved. Part of my fear in receiving more treatment was another long road like we had had with Charlie to fall pregnant again.

I had a very nervous pregnancy, often consumed with fear. Every twinge, pain, or discomfort made me more anxious.

The day of my eight-week scan, I bled. A subchorionic hematoma was the cause. I continued to bleed heavily through to sixteen weeks when I was given a cervical stitch. I found it hard to connect with my growing baby, not knowing what would come of the constant bleeding I was experiencing.

But each scan showed a strong, healthy baby. And were given the all-clear at our anomaly scan at eighteen weeks. Our baby was okay. Our baby—another son—was happy and healthy, and I could finally relax.

I ticked the weeks off in my mind. Oh, the relief when I made it past nineteen weeks! With each week that passed, I became more relaxed and eased into my pregnancy.

At twenty-four weeks, I started experiencing pain. I was told it was likely to be Braxton Hicks. I went to the hospital to be checked out and was reassured there was nothing to worry about and sent home. I was still experiencing discomfort the next day. After an examination and monitoring, I was told I was having contractions.

I was admitted to hospital and given the necessary medication to ease my contractions, as well as steroids and in the days that followed a magnesium infusion. My pregnancy would be seen out in hospital on bed rest.

I was seen by NICU doctors and given statistics and survival rates, horrible things to have worrying at your mind; a conversation no mother wants to have. As the days passed, the survival rates went up and my worry eased, a little.

I was invited to the NICU unit many times to talk to staff and look around. I refused all invitations. I was in denial my baby would be admitted to the ward. To me, visiting meant I would picture my child there and exactly what would happen.

I had in my mind I would make it to term.

At twenty-six weeks and five days, I started bleeding. I was rushed to another hospital, out of our local area, as there were no longer NICU beds at our admitting hospital. I got the last bed in NSW. Next option, interstate to Brisbane.

Our little Hunter Charlie arrived, weighing nine hundred and eight grams, on 15 October 2013. He was born at twenty-seven weeks and one day.

It was a very bittersweet day for me. This day marks Pregnancy and Infant Loss Remembrance Day—a day on which I would remember my little Charlie taken too soon, and celebrate the birth of my newborn son.

Our first meeting was an emotional one. I was excited to finally meet our little Hunter, but feared I would lose him too. He was so tiny. Tubes and the noise of monitors and machinery surrounded him. I was so frightened. His head was the size of a tennis ball and the palms of his hands no bigger than my thumbnail. His tiny fingers were the width of a ring I wore on mine.

He was such a beautiful little boy, a blessing, our miracle. So much like his brother too.

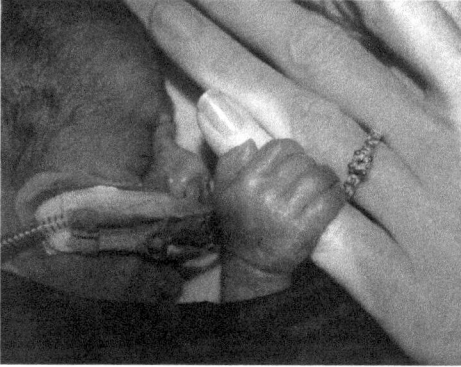

Hunter battled any odds and all the possible outcomes I was told of. He was on CPAP (continuous positive airway pressure) for only three days and then placed on a high flow nasal cannula for respiratory support.

We were told he would, once strong enough in a few weeks, be transferred to a NICU ward closer to home. To our surprise, Hunter was transferred after just nine days from intensive care to the high dependency ward at our local hospital. He was a fighter. He was determined to stay. My many prayers had been answered.

He was the tiniest baby in high dependency at the time.

The NICU journey isn't easy. We were fortunate that Hunter had no major medical complications and grew as he was expected. Apart from a blood transfusion, which is common, he became stronger each day.

The hardest thing was leaving at the end of every day, and grieving for the moments you want as a mother at home with your baby. Instead of waking to a hungry baby, I was expressing every three hours and cried most nights, just wanting him home, in the comfort of our home. NICU was the home away from home for ten weeks.

We were discharged on Christmas Eve of 2013. What a perfect Christmas gift!

We settled into life at home beautifully. Hunter was an easy baby, calm and settled. He was such a blessing; a true little miracle.

There were so many times, looking into Hunter's eyes, I would think of Charlie and miss him even more, knowing I'd missed the same precious moments with him.

I would be consumed with grief at times. I wished he was with us and our boys could be together. I still today would have loved nothing more than to have two little boys running and giggling through the house.

Nothing can prepare you for the emotions that come flooding back when your next child enters the world following a loss, the baby that arrives after the storm, they say, affectionately referred to as a rainbow baby.

For me, it wasn't only grief due to my loss but grief over many things. I didn't get to experience what it was like to be pregnant to term, the swollen ankles, the stretch marks—a reminder of the children I carried—holding my baby after birth, snapping our first family photo in the delivery room with tears of joy in our eyes, breastfeeding from day one, newborn professional photos ...the list goes on.

I would talk about my loss and would be met with silence or words and comments that hurt. Really hurt.

As grieving mothers, all we want is to be heard and be listened to when we find the courage to talk, which isn't easy. To hear words of comfort, for our loss and our babies' short lives. To be validated. To speak of the baby that isn't here, but is still part of our family. To always remember and never forget.

2013 was an intense year. It commenced with heartache with the loss of Charlie but ended in such joy. Our Hunter—our little miracle, our ray of sunshine, our precious rainbow baby—was home. We were finally a family. A family with two boys; one who watches over us and the other a reminder of how precious life really is.

Now, Hunter is a happy and healthy five-year-old boy. I'm beyond proud of him and count my blessings each day. He is smart, funny, affectionate, and social. Those that know him or meet him comment on how endearing he is. He has overcome his own health challenges being born prematurely but has met them with such resilience and bravery. I admire this about Hunter. He is such a beautiful natured, kind, and compassionate child. I feel extremely blessed to be chosen as his mother.

My grief isn't as raw now.

I talk about my loss with more confidence, like I expect to be heard, I guess. I don't shy away from the topic of infant loss. I answer "that" question, "How many children do you have?" with, "Two; one here with me and the other in Heaven," proudly. I don't see the inappropriate comments or reactions to my answers negatively or let them hurt, but rather to raise awareness. To educate those that may appear sheltered from the topic.

In a perfect world, the taboo subject of infant loss would be lifted and allow more women to talk about their experience to help them heal.

I've met so many angel parents over the past six years. Random strangers. To talk openly with another angel parent is comforting. It not only helps you, but you are also validating that person's loss. The feeling you leave them with is that another truly cares for their loss, them. You feel the same. A beautiful moment. Humbling.

I did put my energy into charitable work for a short time, to assist my healing, in a charity providing bereavement gowns to families who had lost a baby. I've held the hands of mothers and grandmothers that have lost their child or grandchild. Spoken at length to many family members over the phone. Sat beside a mother waiting for her preterm baby to arrive. Sat silently, letting them all cry until they're ready to talk. Then listen, holding their hand a little tighter. Left them, leaving behind what would become a significant item in their child's farewell, hoping their pain will ease. Hoping they reach the point I did in my personal journey. Find peace in their recovery. Look back, hoping they feel thought of to this day. All those women and families enter my mind often and the hope too that they are on the other side of intense grief that they were in that moment when we met.

My little Hunter knows about Charlie. That he has a brother in heaven. We do special things in remembrance, chat about him, and visit his resting place. He cuddles his "Charlie Bear" that sits on a rocking chair beside his bed.

He sometimes requests to cuddle him whilst being sung to

sleep. His favourite bedtime song, "Somewhere Over the Rainbow," is sung each evening as he drifts off to sleep. It's a song that brings us both comfort. A song that has such significance to myself and my rainbow baby Hunter, and acknowledges that special little boy that looks over us.

I sing for both of them each night.

I no longer cry when hearing this song, or sing it, as its very much Hunters song too. It has me counting my blessings and is met with a smile as he drifts into slumber.

Life as I know it now is beautiful. The grief has eased, and it does over time. It shifts somehow without even realising it.

"Life is not measured by the breaths we take, but the moments that take our breath away."

Meredith Bale

Meredith Bale, aged forty-four is a single parent and a trained childcare worker. She has a passion for working with children with additional needs.

Meredith's hope is to extend on her experience studying in community services or allied health industry.

Olivia and Rocky

Olivia

You know the saying, "In these moments, time stood still?" Time most definitely stood still on Tuesday, May 20th 2014.

My daughter, Olivia, was born at thirty-three weeks and four days gestation. There was no medical reasoning or conclusion as to why she arrived early; all we were told was that there had been a premature rupture of membranes.

My daughter's due date was July 2nd 2014. We were in the process of renovating our home while we were pregnant with her. I never really did a thing to help as my husband wouldn't let me! He said it was too hard for me and I had to rest. He is one of those men who take everything on and never asks for a single bit of help. He is the most amazing man I have ever known!

My pregnancy was smooth sailing; my blood pressure and blood test results were always perfect; no gestational diabetes, absolutely no issues whatsoever.

I was excited about my baby shower, which was held on Saturday, 17th May. Two days before, I was out shopping with my mum, getting everything we needed. I started to feel exhausted while we were out and we had to end our shopping trip early.

Later that night, I had a really uncomfortable feeling between my legs. It felt like a big bulge was sitting there and I was aching from head to toe. It almost felt like I hadn't sat down in days. My husband sent me to bed with a cup of warm tea and told me to watch TV and not to move.

The next morning, I had a midwife appointment. The midwife I saw was not my usual one; however the student midwife who had been with me the whole journey so far was there. I explained everything I had been feeling and the midwife said I was one hundred percent fine, the baby was nowhere near ready, and they would see me back for my next appointment in two weeks. Boy, were they wrong!

My baby shower was held the following day. I was beyond tired, a feeling I have never felt before. Most of my guests stayed well past the finish time. I was emotional and completely drained. I broke down in tears and said to my sister, "All I want to do is rest. Could you please nicely ask the remaining guests if they could leave?" A finish time that was meant to be 4pm turned into guests not leaving until 9pm! I had a cool shower and went to bed once everyone left.

The following morning, I woke up and felt awful. I remained in bed and slept most of the day.

On Monday, I felt a little bit better. I thought I would start packing my hospital bags—a task that soon proved too tiring and made me quickly sit down. I was back to feeling overly exhausted. I started feeling very anxious and stressed about cleaning, and even though I was tired, all I wanted to do was scrub my kitchen and prepare dinner.

The events to follow are unforgettable. This is where my story begins!

Later that night, I had a warm shower and when I got out, I blow-dried my hair. In the process, I felt a trickle down my leg and my pyjama pants were drenched. I knew I hadn't wet myself; it was a different feeling to passing urine. It was uncomfortable. It would start then stop and start again. I yelled out to my husband and told him to ring the hospital. We told the nurses that I was only at thirty-three weeks gestation, to which they advised me to put a maternity pad on and come in immediately.

A trip to the hospital that took ten minutes felt like half an hour. Once we arrived, we went straight to the birthing suite. I wasn't feeling any pain, just losing more and more fluid. The nurses sent us into the assessment room and checked the fluid I was losing and confirmed active labour. They had neonatal doctors see us and also other doctors whose job was to monitor me if anything went wrong.

There was no real explanation as to why our baby was coming early. There was no turning back. No keeping her in. She was coming!

I was given a steroid injection in my backside to help with our baby's lung development. This was to be given to me again in another twelve hours if I hadn't given birth to her by then. The nurses completed an internal to check if I had dilated at all. I was one centimeter. The doctors advised us that we had to prepare for the worst; however, we didn't really understand their medical jargon. They said that in most cases, babies born at this gestation were okay, however, sometimes things can go wrong and they don't make it. It depended on the baby itself.

As I didn't have pain, I was sent to the antenatal ward. My husband had to leave for the night; he wasn't allowed to stay.

They said they would phone him if he were needed. I have never been so scared in my life. All I wanted at that point was my husband. Between the other patients snoring, strange noises, a dark room, being scared, losing more fluid, and having to pass urine every five to ten minutes, I had no sleep.

Around 3am, I started getting sharp menstrual-like pains in my stomach and asked the nurses for pain relief. They went to get it but never returned. There was a shift change and the previous nurse forgot to advise the current nurse that I needed meds.

Hours passed and I couldn't handle the pain. I asked for pain relief again and told the nurses that the pain was getting worse. They did another internal and I was three centimeters dilated. The nurses decided it was time to go to the birthing suite. All I could think of was my husband. I needed him. He arrived about 9:30am. The date was now Tuesday, 20 May — a day I can never forget.

I received my second steroid injection at 10am. The midwife suggested I start taking the gas for pain relief because I'd started to become uncomfortable. It worked right away, but it didn't last long. Soon I was having continuous contractions without a gap in between, and the midwife suggested I receive an epidural as I wasn't getting a break. I was struggling to breathe. My daughter's heart rate was increasing, and I was told that she could become distressed.

The anesthetist came to speak with me and receive my consent for the needle. But I was in so much pain that I couldn't focus, so I couldn't talk to him. He asked the nurses to check my dilation because he was sure I was too far gone for an epidural. He was correct.

The midwife told me to open my legs and to her surprise, our daughter was crowning! I remember hearing sirens and strange emergency noises. The machines were going crazy!

I could barely open my eyes, but I could faintly see a whole team of people surrounding a big crane-like machine. A female doctor wearing blue scrubs held my hand and talked in my ear, saying, "Only focus on my voice and listen to everything I tell you to do." This woman with her calm, caring manner was my saviour! She was Heaven sent and helped me so much. To this day, I have no idea who she was but I salute her.

After a few pushes and many screams, our little girl was out, born at 12:47pm, weighing 2.008 kilograms and forty-seven centimeters long. She didn't cry as she wasn't breathing. They rushed her to the big crane machine and a whole team of doctors worked on her. All I could do was cry and ask if she was okay. She had tubes everywhere and breathing apparatus on her tiny face. She was rushed out of the room. I told my husband to not worry about me but to stay with our daughter.

This was not the birth I had expected. I expected to hold my baby and cry happy tears. I was exhausted, confused, scared, and lost. The midwife delivered the placenta and told me everything was fine and that I did well.

A room full of people soon attended to me. A midwife came back in and told me to try and have a rest and then they would come back in an hour and get me up for a shower. After an hour, my husband came back to the birthing suite. He had photos of our little girl and said she was fine but needed help with breathing. The midwife asked if I felt well enough to try and get up to have a shower. All I wanted to do was have one! I felt terrible.

Trying to get up off the bed proved difficult and it was very challenging as afterbirth began to seep out. My husband, being the amazing person he is, stayed with me the entire time in the shower so I didn't fall, as I began to feel dizzy. After my shower, the midwife organised a sandwich and a drink for me to give me some energy. Once I finished eating, they asked me to grab my bags and to sit in the wheelchair and they would take me to see my daughter.

In the meantime, my husband's family had arrived. They were extremely excited to see their new addition. She was the first grandchild on my husband's side and the first grand-daughter on my side.

When we arrived at NICU, I realised the seriousness of my daughter's situation. Visitors to the unit were limited and no children were allowed in at all. Even though I was taken aback by the strict rules, I was extremely grateful that the number one priority was the babies. People were kept out to give these vulnerable babies a chance at life.

The room was dark. Ten machines held ten babies. My husband wheeled me to our daughter. My first thought was, *She's so tiny.* Machines and tubes covered her little face and body. Tears rolled down my cheeks. This is the little person who was inside me for all of those months, kicking me and keeping me awake all night. I longed to touch her and as I went to put my hand through the holes in the machine, I was advised not to by a NICU nurse. She said she was far too young and fragile to be touched. Stimulation could increase her heart rate.

I felt like all my rights as her mother were taken away. Being a first-time mum, I already had no idea what to expect but this was a completely unexpected situation. I was then wheeled up to postnatal and given a room. I lay down for a while and then asked my husband to take me down to see our baby again. My heart was pounding and I felt like a little child getting excited over an amusement park. I was so anxious and excited to see our baby—I just felt like running there rather than being wheeled down in a wheelchair.

When we got to the NICU security doors, we were asked for our child's name and the doors were unlocked. There she was—our little princess, sleeping peacefully but still covered in tubes and machines. Never had I seen anything so pure and beautiful in my life.

A lovely nurse introduced herself to us. She said her name was Philippa and she would be looking after our daughter overnight. A sense of relief came over me because I knew she was in good hands. Philippa said, "I know you want to sit here all night and stare at her, but I can tell you're extremely tired. Can I suggest you get some sleep? You can come down any time during the night if you wake up."

My husband said she was right and there was nothing we could do for our baby. She couldn't feed, couldn't be held. There was no point in me being there. All I asked was that if she woke up or cried, could they please call me so I could be there. Philippa agreed.

Going up to my room again made me feel like a piece of me was missing, but I managed to get some sleep. I woke during the night and had to request some pain relief as I started to feel cramps. As soon as the medication kicked in, I was comfortable and got some more sleep. Even though I was waking every two to three hours, I felt okay and somewhat relaxed.

The next day, I got up to freshen myself up a little before my husband arrived. I thought I would go down by myself to see our daughter before he got there. My tiny baby laying there so helpless made me realise how blessed I was to have been given the chance to create such a beautiful little gift.

The nurse came over to me to tell me that her heart rate had dropped overnight but was okay now. Her temperature had also dropped so they had to alter the machines to better incubate her. When my husband arrived, I told him what I had been told. He couldn't stop taking photos; he was just so proud of his baby. The nurse asked if we wanted to touch her and I felt a rush of joy that I could finally make physical contact with my baby.

The little hand sections on the machine were opened and we were told not to stroke her but to place our hands on her back so she could feel us. I felt instant warmth. Then a miracle happened: our daughter opened her eyes and looked at us for the first time. Once again, a tear or two rolled down my cheeks.

I went back up to my room only to be told I was being discharged. My heart sank. I wasn't ready to go home while my baby was in NICU. But the nurses said they needed the bed. I quickly went back down to NICU to tell the nurses I had to leave but I would be back in a couple of hours.

Leaving the hospital was the hardest thing I've ever had to do. I broke down in tears as soon as I got into the car. I was heartbroken. Having to leave my baby just didn't feel right. When we arrived outside our home, the walk up the path to the door was not what I'd imagined. My arms were empty. There was no baby with us. Something that was supposed to be so joyous and full of happiness was not. I cried again as soon as we walked through the front door.

I had a shower so I could get back to the hospital. When we arrived, we realised our baby had been placed into another machine with the blue UV light due to jaundice. She still had CPAP equipment for oxygen, and tubes and wires galore. The nurses said she had jaundice, but it was common and not to worry. As I had previously seen jaundice first hand with my nephews, I wasn't too alarmed by it and knew it was under control. She also had to be given antibiotics via IV drip for fluid the doctors had found on her lungs.

I began expressing colostrum so the nurses could tube feed our baby. It was only a half to one milliliter, but it was liquid gold! It was all new to me. It was extremely difficult to bring in my milk. Emotions were running wild. I was tired, stressed, and didn't know what to do when it came to expressing. But I did what I could.

I cried a lot around this time—at least five times a day. I started to feel strange. I didn't feel like I had a connection to my child. I wanted to be a normal mother, one who could hold her baby.

But we saw Olivia grow a little bit each day. When she was four days old, I was asked if I wanted to hold her. I watched the nurses open the incubator and hold all the tubes and wires while one of them placed her on my chest. Instant warmth and comfort is the only way to describe the feeling I felt. I tear up as I write this because it's a feeling that I will never forget, the first time I had actually felt like a mother. That was the moment I felt the connection. It was an instant love. Before this, I had loved my daughter but there was something missing. As soon as I held her, this all changed. I was in love. She was mine, and I was hers. I would do anything to protect her.

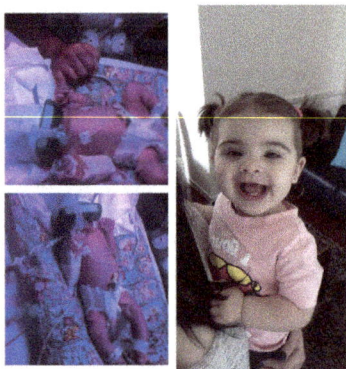

The days went on and she progressed well. Every three hours, I would be there for nappy changes, cleaning her down with a saline solution, tube feeds, cuddles, singing her lullabies and most importantly Kangaroo Care. I was on top of the world. Spending time in NICU wasn't the vision I originally had when I was pregnant with her, but it would do—as long as I had her.

One day, I returned to the hospital and could not find my baby. I frantically searched for her until a nurse asked which baby I was looking for and I said, "Olivia Panetta." She laughed and said, "It's okay, she has been moved to bay four." I sighed with relief. Bay four was where babies were placed when they were almost ready to go home.

I rushed to bay four. There she was, patiently waiting with her little eyes open, staring around the room. She was out of her incubator and in a normal crib/ bassinet on wheels. She still had wires and tubes attached to her. The doctor came and told me she was doing great and that it was feed and grow from here on in. I was so happy I couldn't wipe the smile off my face.

A couple of days passed and we were trying to latch her to feed; however she just couldn't suck. The nurses told me that babies learn the sucking technique around thirty-six weeks gestation. She had not reached this stage yet. Tube feeding while she leant up against my breast was the way to encourage her. She tried a little bit but would fall asleep while sucking.

Another day passed and my husband and I couldn't be happier with how our little girl was growing. I walked into NICU all smiles, only to have it quickly wiped off my face. The doctors were hovering over my baby. They told me that her heart rate jumped then dropped. They also heard a heart murmur. This was all new language to me. I didn't know what a heart murmur was. They said they were organising for a cardiologist from Westmead Children's Hospital to check her. He would be there later on in the day. I sat by her side and did not move. The day passed and the specialist never showed up.

This was when I met Kate, a nurse I will never forget. She introduced herself and said it was a good sign that he hadn't shown up yet because it meant they didn't believe it was urgent. She reassured me everything was going to be okay. The day ended and I was emotional once again.

The next day, I went back into the hospital and sat and waited for the specialist. This time, he showed up! He listened to her heart and checked reports and said absolutely no heart murmur could be heard. He said it might have been an error in the machinery. What a relief!

Then my world came crashing down once again. I walked in one morning and saw my daughter turned on her belly, bottom in the air and a light on her back. No nappy on. I looked closely and saw a hole in the base of her spine, almost where her tailbone is but lower down towards her bottom. It was something I had never seen before. I asked the nurse what had happened and she replied, "I'm so sorry, I cannot discuss this with you. I have to get the doctor." My heart began to race with fear and I felt sick.

The doctor approached me calmly and said, "Hello, Mrs. Panetta. I have just been told you wanted to speak with me about your daughter." I asked him what the hole was on the base of her spine. He told me it was a sacral dimple and they had ordered an ultrasound to be performed on it. He explained that a sacral dimple was associated with Spina Bifida. The ultrasound would determine how deep the sacral dimple was and whether she did have Spina Bifida.

The doctor carried on talking but I couldn't hear a thing. The room was spinning, my heart was racing, and I held back tears. When he stopped speaking, all I could stammer out was, "But she's kicking her legs!" and he agreed that was a good sign. I left the room after the doctor had gone, as I couldn't hold back tears. I called my husband, hysterical. He was at work but I asked him to come quickly as I needed him. I couldn't be there alone.

The day passed, and the following day the scan was done. I

was shaking as the doctors approached us. They said the scan was clear and confirmed that even though she did indeed have a sacral dimple, it was not deep enough to diagnose Spina Bifida in any way. They said she might experience lower back pain in later life, but was otherwise a healthy little child. The tears this time were happy ones.

A week went by and then another. Our little girl was growing beautifully. She had a head full of hair and big brown eyes. She looked premature still but she was perfect. However, my milk dried up and I couldn't express at all. I felt like a failure. The nurse who I will cherish forever, Kate, reminded me that as long as Olivia was getting food and growing, I was doing a great job.

Kate suggested we try formula. I was hesitant, but as soon as we gave her the bottle, Olivia latched onto the teat and sucked away. She drank almost the whole bottle and instantly fell asleep. She was satisfied after her big feed. The days went on and we continued with the formula. She grew and grew. We were over the moon!

The NICU began to feel like a second home. We knew all the nurses and some of the other mums and dads. One morning, I came into the hospital as usual and the head registrar came and sat beside me and asked if we were ready to take Olivia home. I said, "I cannot wait until we get to take her home. It's everything I have been waiting for." She then said, "I think she's ready to go home today." My eyes lit up and I couldn't stop smiling. The head registrar said the doctors just had to check Olivia and confirm she was okay to leave and then we would be discharged. I raced home and packed a going home outfit and lots of blankets, as the day was freezing cold.

I arrived back at the hospital and found the doctors in the room. They said she was ready to go home. The nurses all had smiles on their faces and wished us well. The doctors asked us to bring her back in three days so they could check her to make sure she was gaining weight and that all was okay.

Suddenly, a loud scream and wailing broke into our happiness. I jumped and immediately looked towards the door of our bay. Nurses and doctors surrounded another mother and father, trying to console them and hold them up. They had just lost their baby. My heart broke for them. Even though I was happy that I was taking my daughter home, I couldn't help but feel terribly sad and angry at the world for taking that little baby away. I still think about that family to this day and remember their screams and cries. These sounds will stick in my mind forever and I don't think they will ever leave.

Olivia is now a happy, healthy and smart four and-a-half-year-old little girl. She amazes me every single day. She teaches me new things. She has taught me to be the best person I can be. She has taught me to love wholeheartedly and never give up. The strength and determination that my little warrior has shown since the second she was born makes me the proudest mum in the world. I love this little girl with everything I have!

Rocky

After Olivia was born, we have since added a little boy to our family, Rocky James Panetta. Boy oh boy, is he an active, fun, loving, and strong little man.

Rocky also had a hard start to life. I was high risk my whole pregnancy due to the complications surrounding Olivia's birth and the unknown. We still to this day have no conclusion as to what actually caused Olivia to arrive prematurely.

Rocky arrived at forty weeks plusone day gestation. A normal entrance to the world, a hard one, but normal!

I was tested at thirty-six weeks for GBS. Results came back positive. So as they do, nurses administered antibiotics during labour.

I felt instant love with Rocky; his was the way "normal" births and deliveries go. I held him in my arms after he came out, staring into his little eyes. This was the birth I'd longed for.

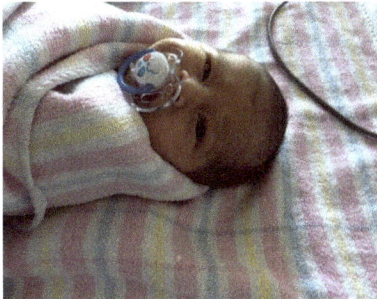

We were discharged the following day, going home as a family of four. We were all so smitten and in love with our new addition. Olivia took to him so well and loved her new role as big sister.

A week went by; we were tired but loving life. Then day ten came along. I noticed Rocky would not wake up to feed and he was extremely fatigued. Even though he was my second child, I put it down to just being tired and adjusting to his new life on the outside world. My parents came over for a visit that afternoon; I still remember it was 2pm. My dad was so excited to see both kids and really wanted to hold Rocky. I said he had been sleeping a lot and my dad said he should be due for a feed and to get him up.

As I picked him up and handed him to my dad, he said, "My god, he is hot."

I touched his tiny head and he was burning up. I grabbed the digital thermometer and checked his temperature—it read thirty-eight point seven degrees Celsius. My stomach turned and I ran for my phone straight away, calling the hospital maternity ward as we were still under their care until day fourteen. The nurse said, "Rush him straight to emergency and advise them you have already phoned us."

I hate to admit it, but I don't think I have ever driven so fast in my life. I just knew something was wrong.

I ran into emergency with his tiny limp body in my arms; he was deteriorating so rapidly. The administration lady said something straight away to the triage nurse, and she opened the door right away and rushed us straight through to resus. An alarm was pushed and within minutes, emergency doctors were standing there and advised me they also had paediatric doctors on their way.

I was asked a series of questions about the birth, his gestation, were any medications administered while in labour? I said, "Yes, antibiotics for GBS." The doctors kept trying to place a canular into his small little hand, but he was so weak they couldn't get the vein. They tried and tried and finally got one. They drew blood out to test urgently. All I could do was watch as they worked on my baby.

In my mind, all I could think of was *Please God, not again.*

The doctors began to speak amongst themselves and ordered a chest X-ray immediately, suspecting pneumonia. They checked the screen as it was being performed and said it was clear. They then placed me into a wheelchair holding Rocky in my arms with wires and needles everywhere and rushed us up to Children's Ward, advising me along the way that I needed to give consent for them to perform a Lumbar puncture.

I still remember saying, "I am sorry, what is that?"

A lumbar puncture: *"the procedure of taking fluid from the spine in the lower back through a hollow needle, usually done for diagnostic purposes."*

He was taken from my arms and rushed away. They advised me that I could not be present as it is a very confronting procedure and they do not recommend parents be there.

After one hour, he was brought into a room in Children's Ward, and it was then that we were advised by a nurse that we were being placed into isolation and we had to remain there until the results were back. She said the doctors would come and see us shortly.

When the doctors arrived, they got to the point quite promptly. "We are suspecting meningitis."

Until you hear those words come out of a doctor's mouth about your own child, any form of fear you have ever felt before is laughable. The way I felt right then in that moment was indescribable fear! My eyes filled with tears, I could barely stand. The doctors advised us that we both had to stay the night as it was going to be touch and go and he may not make it through the night. I could barely breathe as I looked over to my husband who had arrived and his eyes showed his fear, filling with tears. This is a man that never shows fear, sadness, or pain. EVER! In that moment, we both knew this was serious.

Rocky was brought back to us and placed into a cot in the middle of this big room. It was so quiet, dark, and scary. We just sat there and watched our little helpless baby fight to live. He was breathing so fast, his temperature spiking to forty point six degrees Celsius. He was attached to fluids and IV antibiotics.

We didn't sleep at all that night. Our minds raced, and we watched and prayed, also thinking of our little girl at home who needed us. Thank God for grandparents! We knew she was safe and happy.

The next morning, doctors confirmed the fluid taken showed meningitis and also a severe UTI.

Day two was just as intense as day one. We remained in hospital for another four days. He improved tremendously and we were discharged.

A few more days went past, and I still remember, it was 5:20am. I got his bottle ready to feed him and his breathing was so bad. So fast and loud! I ripped open his onesie and immediately saw visible recessions. My husband had left for work already, and I rang him to say, "Come back home now or I'm calling 000 for an ambulance." He was home within minutes, and we arrived at emergency not long after.

Again, he was rushed through to resus. A canular was placed into his foot this time as he was black and blue from his hospital stay just days before. The doctors took blood to test so they could confirm what was happening. Again, we were placed into isolation as they could not risk anyone else being infected had it been meningitis. They ruled out meningitis and confirmed it was bronchiolitis and RSV/Rhinovirus.

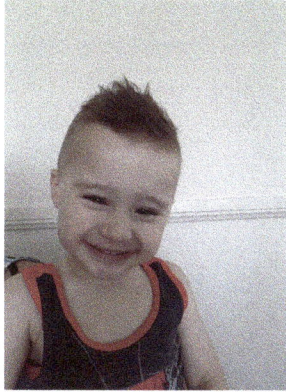

Our whole world once again felt like it was crumbling. He was placed on oxygen to support his breathing as his levels were low. He received fluids via IV, and we were told to lower his feeds as feeding could interfere with his breathing. We remained in hospital for five days and he showed a lot of improvement. We were discharged and sent home to once again be a family of four.

I wanted to not only share Olivia's story but also Rocky's, to raise awareness on GBS. It is a real thing! Streptococcal Infection Group B is serious. If your baby is showing any of the signs that Rocky did, please, *please* get them to a hospital. We are lucky to have him alive today.

Some people don't realise how lucky they are to have healthy babies, or better yet to be given the chance to carry a baby without any difficulty. There are families out there who would long to have a baby but can't. Families that wish they could take their babies home and live happily ever after, but that isn't the case for some.

During our NICU experience, we saw newborn babies being brought out of addictions to Ice and other drugs that their mothers took while pregnant with them. There was another child who was alone day in and day out—his mum left and never returned for him. I had to witness this tiny, innocent baby be signed over to the state as no family wanted him.

Another child had a mother that used to come once a week wearing green prison wear. And a decent, loving family lost their baby. These memories will stick with us forever. We are grateful for everything that Nepean NICU did for us. They will forever be a part of our family.

Natalie Panetta

My name is Natalie Panetta. I'm a twenty-nine-year-old mother of two beautiful children. I am married to my amazing husband Carmelo of five years. I'm a stay-at-home mum and enjoy spending each and every moment with my kids.

I have just recently started my own business creating individual dessert cups for events, parties, and wholesale. I am still in the early stages however my goal is to expand my business and be as successful as I can be to ensure my children's future is secure and set up financially.

My goal in life is to be happy and healthy. Without happiness and health, what else is there? I am who I am, and do what I do every day for my two little blessings. They are my life.

Emilee

"This isn't the type of thing that happens to me."

"You hear of other people going through this, but I'm not one of those women."
"This isn't real. This wasn't supposed to happen."

I lost count of how many different ways I had said the same thing. I'd heard of stillbirth, of course. But stillbirth wasn't supposed to happen to me.

It was when my midwife started exchanging awkward glances with the other midwife in the room; I realised I'd repeated the same phrase over and again … and again. It was time for me to stop talking.

I was twenty weeks and four days pregnant. I'd been in hospital for four days. Every ultrasound had shown a healthy baby—our third baby girl. Every check with the Doppler had given us a healthy heartbeat to listen to. But last night, things had changed. My bleeding had gotten even worse. Small contraction-like feelings came and went with building intensity. I put my prayers out to the universe and hoped like hell my little girl would hold on.

I'd even looked at the clock at 11:11 and knew it must be a positive sign.
"We think you should call your husband to come back up," they'd told me a few hours earlier after labour was obvious. And here he now stood, holding my hand, as he had my other labours, this time with a different kind of tension. He wasn't letting go.

"Have you thought of a name?" We had to name her? We had to name her. She needed to know she'd been loved from the start. She needed to belong. I needed her to belong. And for that to happen, I needed to let her let go.

"Emilee. But with two E's." And unlike any time we'd had a similar conversation before, Michael agreed immediately.

"I think it's time, Carolyn. It's time to deliver your little girl," my midwife, Karen, said gently. "When you're ready. But it's time to meet her."

I'm not sure what I was expecting, but to me at that time, the pain was just as intense as either of my other labours. I needed to rock. I needed to kneel up. I needed to feel like I was in a "proper" labour. Physically, the relief at the end was the same too. The difference was the agonising silence. No crying baby. No congratulatory sayings. No pats on the back for the happy dad.

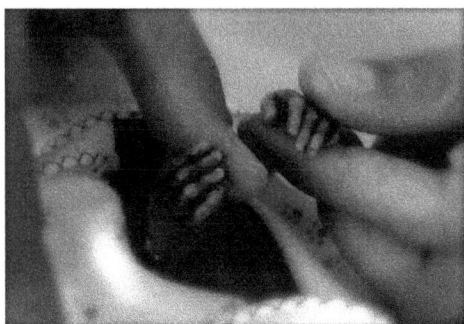

Karen, who two weeks earlier had been a stranger, now became one of the most significant people in our world. As she placed our tiny bundle on my chest and asked Michael if he wanted to cut the umbilical cord, she put her hand on me and told us how beautiful our daughter was. Over the next few hours, she ensured that we made as many memories as a family as possible. She knew what words to say and guided us in what to say to others. She took photos and footprints. And her care with our little girl was always gentle and precious. I truly believe that our experience in hospital would've been completely different if not for her by our side.

The next day and a half was a blur. Emilee stayed with us the whole time. Confusion set in and I found I didn't really know how to act. I wanted to hold her as much as possible, but was that weird? I wanted to put her in the cot while I slept or went to the bathroom, but did that mean I didn't want to hold her? I could hear the motor of the cold cot running. How did that make me feel? The midwives had put a little gown on her and I thought it was ugly. Was that ridiculous? I needed to put a blanket over her body. But was that to make me feel better or to stop visitors from looking at her?

As family came and went, I felt numb. I didn't want to grieve in front of some of them. Others didn't want to grieve in front of me. Lots of whispering happened around me. And I let it. Michael, my mum, and my sister filtered calls, made the important decisions, and got me ready to leave hospital—without Emilee—to come home with one less daughter.

For a long time after her birth, the moment we walked out that door and left Emilee in the arms of Karen was the hardest. The next hardest was leaving the cemetery on the day of her funeral. I felt like I was walking away on her. As silly as it sounds, in those moments, I felt like I was betraying her.

Our life was different now. I thought of life in two stages: Before Emilee and After Emilee. I felt worried rather than excited when I heard other people were pregnant. I often felt like I had to force myself to be happy, or at least not to show sadness (and mostly because it made other people feel bad). And we spoke about death with our girls—often.

If there's anything in this whole process that I feel proud of, it's the way we have dealt with the loss with Jasmine and Ava. From meeting their sister in a cold hospital room to involving them in the funeral arrangements by choosing their favourite coloured balloons to asking a thousand times why Emilee couldn't stay with us, we have been nothing but honest with them. I think that many people often disregard how resilient children can be. We are proud that we are raising two girls who look at death sensitively, realistically, and with a genuine sense of how long forever is.

For a long time after Emilee's stillbirth, Jasmine, nearly four at the time, asked questions constantly. She missed her baby sister with a love that she couldn't understand. She wanted to know why the doctors couldn't make her better, why she couldn't stay in Mummy's tummy, and still now is very perceptive when people around her are upset.

I am also proud of the way Ava, then eighteen months (now five), pulls me up when talking about our family members. One of the trickiest questions I get asked is, "How many children do you have?"… Well, obviously I have three, but to the person who only knows me with two, or the person I've just met, or someone I haven't seen for a while, do I really need to go into our story? If Ava is with me—yes I do. Otherwise, she corrects me. She freely talks about her little sister and tells people that Mummy had a baby that died. She draws pictures for Emilee. Tells her new friends about her and includes her name on things like raffle tickets and Melbourne Cup sweeps!

February 23 is the most emotional day of our year. On her first birthday, we wanted to remember Emilee appropriately and I really wanted it to be perfect. I had planned to have a picnic, release a rainbow of balloons and spend the day peacefully. Just as it did the day of her funeral, it poured with rain. So the picnic was out, the balloons didn't fly into the sky, and we ended up heading into the local shopping centre and playing arcade games with noisy teenagers. It tore me apart, and I hated it.

I realised afterwards that I had put too much emphasis on it being perfect. I realised it wasn't going to be the perfect day I wanted it to be without Emilee to blow out the candles. We decided then that Emilee's birthday would become our Family Day. So we make it a day the girls will remember. Whether it's roller-skating, ferry rides, trips to Luna Park, chocolate and pancakes for dinner, or playing in the park, we plan to always fondly remember the day that Emilee came to us. There is the rest of the year to be upset that she didn't get to stay— but her birthday—that's for fun!

Shortly before Emilee's birth, I had begun making personalised candles for family and friends and the day before I was admitted to hospital, I had completed my first order for a perfect stranger, thanks to the world of Facebook. In the weeks after Emilee's birth, my inbox slowly filled with new orders and I began to immerse myself in choosing the right wording, the correct ribbon colour and embellishments so that I could create something special for other people. The candles were for christenings and weddings—special milestones that I would never be able to celebrate with my little girl.

Creating the candles gave me space. Michael would take the girls away while I worked, or I worked while the girls were in childcare and school. My music played and I created special keepsakes. And I cried, even when I was excited to have a new project. It became my therapy. It also became my serendipity. Something that almost felt like it was meant to be, but could only be because I'd lost Emilee.

"Serendipity: the effect by which one accidentally stumbles upon something fortunate…
Especially while looking for something entirely unrelated."

From these first orders, a business grew: Serendipity Event Candles. The next couple of years were consumed with creating candles and other personalised items to help create special memories for other families. Before long, our home was so cluttered with candles and all the paraphernalia that went along with it that we decided to move to a bigger house so that we could give my business the best shot. It had changed from my therapy to trying to make money.

Outwardly, I was confident. I attended wedding expos, advertised locally, and set up a website, deciding to build a business for myself, my family, and in memory of our baby girl. Running the business gave me confidence and the strength that I needed to show everyone I was coping. It was also nerve-racking. With every few steps forward, I'd fall back a little, trying to perfect my product because it was a reflection on me. On Emilee's memory.

Serendipity Event Candles was getting to the stage where I couldn't cope with the workload and started to look into hiring help. It was now taking so much of my time that it also needed to prove itself financially. This is where it ended. In a way, that I found difficult to explain to others, the guilt that I had with the business overwhelmed me.

One night, sitting down to about a dozen different projects and applying for a new wedding expo, I fell to pieces and realised why I hadn't pushed my business growth earlier. I was making money off Emilee's stillbirth. As serendipitous as I had been treating it, I realised that I had felt guilt in benefiting from her death. And I couldn't cope with that.

All at once, relief took over. I realised I no longer needed Serendipity Event Candles. I had begun to resent endless phone calls with customers who insisted the print wasn't right or I'd used the wrong font or the ribbon was a shade too dark. My grief had come to a point where I didn't need all this. I was ready to close that door. Start a new chapter. I had worked through the most difficult part of my grief with my hands, and they were now going to be able to rest. I had kept myself so busy and would now be able to spend more time with my girls and cherish them that little bit more. And that was where I needed to be in that moment. In a similar way to Emilee's birth, it was time for me to let that part of my grief go.

Fast forward, and you'll find us here—just over four years After Emilee. Life is tough, and everyone has their struggles. This is ours. It makes us who we are. Our little blessing has taught us resilience; has taught us that life doesn't always make sense and we don't always find out the answers. Loss changes you and that's okay. So it should. We didn't get here without hard work.

We find courage where we need it, love in those around us, and comfort in each other.

Emilee will always be a part of our story. We have promised each other nothing less.

Carolyn Viera

My name is Carolyn Viera. I am mum to Jasmine, Ava & Emilee. I am wife to Michael. I am a primary school teacher and small business owner.

Writing my story about Emilee's stillbirth was a turning point in my grief, and I am forever thankful for the experience.

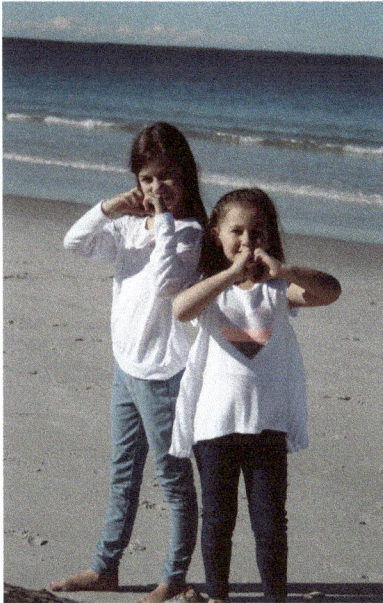

An Afterword from Melissa

Dear parents and families,

I'm sorry that you've been through heartache through pregnancy. I'm sorry that you've had to experience this unforgettable, life changing, heartbreaking time in your life when it's meant to be joyful. I'm sorry that your pregnancy and pregnancy struggle didn't go to plan.

I do want to thank you for reading these beautiful and heart-warming memoirs to help you feel comfort through your tears and I do hope that in some way, they have brought you hope, support, guidance, love, and assurance that you're not alone.

To all the writers, thank you from the bottom of my heart for dedicating your time to write your memoir for this book with so much courage. I hope writing has been a healing experience for you.

If you've read *Comfort for the Tears, Light for the way*, you may recall some of the stories. You may have noticed, however, that many have extended their families or their life has changed in a positive way. This can be you too.

I believe that writing about part of your life can change your life. It did for me, and I'm sure that many opportunities from now will come your way.

Start or keep writing and share it with the world. Don't be afraid. Let your emotions flow through your words and show the people that need to know how you feel by sharing your story with them.

With love, Melissa

About the Author

Melissa Desveaux is a mother of four angels and two boys, Damien and Ethan, has lived in Sydney Australia her whole life and works as a debt officer in the public service.

She enjoys spending time with her children, writing, creating books and helping writers achieve their dream to become self-published authors.

Melissa's experience with loss has given her the courage and strength to share her story so that families with a similar experience will know that they are not alone.

Her business Melissa Desveaux - Self-Publishing Consulting was foundered in 2018, after a need for help from authors wanting to write and self-publish their own book.

Melissa's mission is to help people write their personal story and get it published so they too can share it with the people that may need to read it.

You can contact Melissa through Facebook - Melissa Desveaux or website - melissadesveaux.com

Join the Facebook Groups:
Write-Self-Publish-Empower - Community for Inspiring Authors

Join the Pregnancy Trauma Support Community

Support & Resources

There are many organistaions around the world that can support families relating to pregnancy or infant loss, Premature babies or IVF so please reach out to them if you need support.

Listed here are a few for your reference.

Life's Little Treasures Foundation

At Life's Little Treasures Foundation, our number one priority is offering support and information to families of premature and sick babies. We do this in many ways ranging from in hospital support to a 24 hour support line, we produce comprehensive information booklets and run an oversubscribed financial assistance program to name just a few of our programs. We also maintain a comprehensive website which includes details of books relevant to parents of premature and sick babies.

www.lifeslittletreasures.org.au
contact_us@lifeslittletreasures.org.au

Little Silk Wings

Little Silk Wings run events around Australia called Let Me See My Baby, designed for professionals and community to learn ways of responding to the death of a baby that are filled with compassion and dignity.

www.littlesilkwings.com.au

-

Bears of Hope

Bears of Hope pregnancy & infant loss support provides leading support and exceptioinal care for families who have experienced the loss of their baby.
We seek to provide crucial information and embrace families during their difficult time of loss and beyond. Families receive a Bear of Hope donated by another bereaved family. This allows the donating family to give their childs brief life purpose and lasting legacy, whilst filling the empty arms of another family as they walk out of hospity without their baby.

www.bearsofhope.org.au
Contact@bearsofhope.org.au

The Compassionate Friends, UK

Support for bereaved parents and their families after the death of a child of any age and from any cause.

www.tcf.org.uk
Helpline on 0345 123 2304 (UK)
helpline@tcf.org.uk

The Miscarriage Association

The Miscarriage Association is a UK-wide charity that offers support and information for anyone affected by miscarriage, ectopic pregnancy or molar pregnancy.

www.miscarriageassociation.org.uk
01924200799 UK
info@miscarriageassociation.org.uk

The Stillbirth Foundation

The only Australian charity dedicated to stillbirth research and we are 100 percent community funded. Since our foundation in 2005, the Stillbirth Foundation has allocated over $1million to funding the most rigorously designed studies aimed at finding a means of preventing stillbirth and supporting the families of stillborn babies.

www.stillbirthfoundation.org.au

Sands

Provides support, information and education to anyone affected by the death of a baby before, during or shortly after birth.

www.sands.org.au
support@sands.org.au

Red Nose

Offers free bereavement support services to anyone impacted by the heartbreaking sudden unexpected death of a baby or child including miscarriage, medical termination, stillbirth and neonatal death.

www.rednose.com.au
Support service line - 1300 308 307

Australian Multiple Birth Association

Australia's leading charity for twins, triplets and more. On our site you will find tips about what to expect while you are pregnant, information on common issues for multiple birth, and there is useful information if you are already a multiple birth family.

www.amba.org.au

Angel Gowns Australia

Provide Angel Gown garments that have been lovingly transformed from donated wedding dresses for families when they are faced with the unimaginable loss of their baby or child.

www.angelgownsaustralia.org
enquiry@angelgownsaustralia.org.au

Faith makes all things possible

Love makes all things easy

Hope makes all things work

·

www.ingramcontent.com/pod-product-compliance
Lightning Source LLC
Chambersburg PA
CBHW041820090426

42811CB00009B/1052